gna roasted

dumplings

d casserole

eatloaf pie

ew braised

e ribs soup

P9-DCQ-252

the
slow cooking
book

Published by Fog City Press
814 Montgomery Street
San Francisco, CA 94133 USA

Copyright © 2002 Weldon Owen Pty Ltd
Reprinted 2002, 2003

Chief Executive Officer: John Owen
President: Terry Newell
Publisher: Lynn Humphries
Managing Editor: Janine Flew
Art Director: Kylie Mulquin
Editorial Coordinator: Tracey Gibson
Editorial Assistant: Kiren Thandi
Production Manager: Caroline Webber
Production Coordinator: James Blackman
Sales Manager: Emily Jahn
Vice President International Sales: Stuart Laurence
European Sales Director: Vanessa Mori

Project Editor: Lynn Cole
Project Designer: Jacqueline Richards
Food Photography: Valerie Martin
Food Stylist: Sally Parker
Home Economist: Christine Sheppard
Recipe Development: Michelle Earl

All rights reserved. Unauthorized reproduction, in any manner, is prohibited.
A catalog record for this book is available from the Library of Congress, Washington, DC.

ISBN 1 876778 99 7

Color reproduction by SC (Sang Choy) International Pte Ltd
Manufactured by Kyodo Printing Co. (S'pore) Pte Ltd
Printed in Singapore

A Weldon Owen Production

the
slow cooking
book

FOG CITY PRESS

contents

introduction

As a technique for making the tougher cuts of meat tender and palatable, slow cooking has been around since our ancestors first dragged home wild game to feed their families. Pots simmered away over camp fires and the meat that emerged was succulent and easily digested, with a warming soup as a bonus that made the meat go further. Later on, busy village-dwellers favored casseroles that could be prepared well ahead of mealtimes and left alone to cook, often in the local baker's cooling oven, while the housewife attended to her other chores.

In some societies, food is still slow-cooked over the remains of a fire built in a pit in the ground. The food—meat, chicken, fish, and many kinds of vegetables—is well-wrapped in large leaves and packed into the pit over the fire's dying embers. Earth is then pushed in over the food to keep the heat in and the oven is left undisturbed for several hours. If you are lucky enough ever to share a feast produced in this way, it's an experience you will not quickly forget.

Another variant of this technique is the haybox, in which the dish is brought to the boil, covered with a tight-fitting lid, and the pot is enclosed inside a box well-insulated with a thick lining of hay or other insulating material. The food, perhaps a rich stew of meat and vegetables, continues to cook gently in the residual heat for several hours.

In the 1970s, electric slow cookers moved into the kitchen in a big way, with busy working mothers finding the convenience of having a meal already cooked when they arrived home in the evening well worth spending a few extra minutes of preparation in the morning. The latest slow cookers are now easier than ever to use and are enjoying a new wave of popularity as another generation of cooks discovers their many advantages.

what are the benefits of slow cooking?

First, with casseroles, pot roasts, slow-baked roasts, and slow cookers, there's no need for constant attention or stirring to stop your dish from burning. And your meal won't be spoiled by overcooking if there's a short delay at serving time.

When guests are invited, there's no last-minute rush. You have plenty of time to attend to other things while the meal takes care of itself.

Economise on cost, but not on flavor, by using tougher, less expensive cuts of meat. A long cooking time ensures that they will be tender and succulent.

a few points to remember ...

With slow cookers, keep the lid on as much as possible to prevent loss of precious heat. The cooker can take as long as 20 minutes to regain the heat lost when you remove the lid to stir the contents or to add more ingredients, so work quickly and get the lid back on as soon as you can.

Manufacturers recommend that slow cookers should be half to three-fourths full for best results. And remember that even though a slow cooker is switched on for several hours, it consumes very little power, so it's a very economical mode of cooking.

Go easy on salt during cooking. As the liquid evaporates, the saltiness can intensify and you can't take out the extra salt. It's better to taste the dish at the end of cooking time and add more salt or other seasonings then, if necessary.

to clean your slow cooker...

Follow the manufacturer's instructions. To make cleanup easier, spray your slow cooker with nonstick food spray before adding the food. Use wooden spoons for stirring, so as not to damage the surface of your slow cooker—food may stick to a damaged area.

experiment with slow cooking...

With a little planning, two or more courses can be cooking at the same time, saving you fuel costs and time on washing up.

the basics of
slow cooking

Read the whole recipe before you start cooking so that you know you have all the utensils and ingredients you need. Use one chopping board for raw meat and poultry, and a separate one for cutting up fruits, vegetables, and other foods. Surprisingly, vegetables often take longer to cook in a slow cooker than meats, so follow the directions in the recipe as to the size the vegetables are to be cut. If they are cut into small, thin pieces and placed near the bottom or sides of the slow cooker, they should cook properly in the time suggested by the recipe. Always wash chopping boards and utensils in hot soapy water after use.

Once the dish is cooked, don't leave it sitting in the slow cooker with the heat turned off for too long. Food must be kept hotter than 140°F (60°C) or cooler than 40°F (4°C) to prevent the growth of harmful bacteria. If the food is not to be eaten straight away, transfer it to a clean container, cover, and refrigerate as soon as possible. Do not reheat in the slow cooker. Use a microwave oven, the range top, or the oven to reheat the dish.

As you get used to cooking in this time-honored way, you may wish to adapt some of your family's favorite dishes to this method. Try to find a similar recipe in this book or in the booklet that came with your slow cooker. Note the quantity and size of the meat and vegetable pieces and the cooking times. Because the slow cooker retains moisture better than other methods, you may need to reduce the amount of liquid in the recipe by up to half. Add dairy products at the end of cooking so they don't curdle.

selecting the right meat Choose the tougher inexpensive cuts for slow-cooked dishes. They will be fork-tender, but will hold their shape better than more expensive roasting or grilling cuts. Another bonus is that they are usually leaner, so you will be cutting down on fat. Truss or joint poultry so that it's easier to handle.

trussing poultry and game birds Tuck the neck flap under the folded wings at the back. Place a piece of cotton string across the bird with the centre of the string just below the breastbone. Bring the string down over the wings to cross underneath, then bring the ends up to tie the legs and the tail securely together.

jointing poultry and game birds Place the bird, breast side up, on a chopping board and cut off the wing tips at the last joint. Pull one leg away from the body and, using a large, sharp knife, cut through the skin and flesh between the body and the thigh until the knife comes to the ball and socket joint. Holding the leg firmly, twist

and bend it outwards until the ball of the thigh bone pops from the socket. Continue to cut off the leg through the flesh. Repeat with the other leg. If you wish, cut the drumstick from the thigh where the thigh bone joins the leg bone. Holding the bird firmly upright with the neck end on the board, cut halfway down through the ribs to separate the breast and wings from the back part of the carcass. Pull the breast away from the remaining part of the back and cut through the skin at the neck. Lay the breast on the board, skin side up, and cut in half lengthwise. Tap the back of the knife with a heavy kitchen weight to make cutting through the bone easier.

jointing a rabbit If the rabbit comes with kidneys and liver, remove them first. Put the rabbit, belly side down, on a board. Pull the hind legs out and away from the body and cut through the hip joints to remove them. Remove the forelegs by cutting between the collarbone and the backbone. Using poultry shears, trim the body at both ends, then trim the skin flaps at the sides. Cut the body (saddle) across in halves.

the importance of using good stock

Homemade stock adds richness and flavor to soups, stews, casseroles, and sauces. Stock can be purchased, but although this is convenient and can be good, it is not as good as homemade. Stock cubes can be used, but they may contain monosodium glutamate and other synthetic flavorings. Bought stock or stock cubes usually contain salt, but if you make your own stock with little or even no salt, you will have better control over the saltiness of the finished dish.

beef stock Heat 1 tablespoon olive oil in a stockpot or large saucepan and brown 3 lb (1.5 kg) beef bones all over. Add 1 medium onion, peeled and quartered, and 1 lb (500 g) shin beef and brown slowly. Add 8 cups (2 qt/2 l) water and bring very slowly to the boil, then add 1 cup (8 fl oz/250 ml) of cold water and reduce the heat.

Skim any scum from the surface, then add 1 medium carrot, peeled and sliced, 1 rib (stick) celery, trimmed and chopped, and 1 bouquet garni. Partly cover the stockpot with a lid and simmer over low heat for 5–6 hours, skimming the scum frequently from the surface of the stock. Strain the stock through a colander lined with a piece of muslin or a clean tea towel. Cool and refrigerate the stock overnight. Next day, carefully discard the solidified fat from the surface. Stock can be frozen for later use.

makes about 10 cups (2½ qt/2.5 l)

vegetable stock Peel and slice 2 medium carrots and 2 large onions. Heat 3 tablespoons olive oil in a large stainless-steel or enamel saucepan and cook the vegetables for 2–3 minutes. Add 2 large, ripe tomatoes, chopped, 3 ribs (sticks) celery, trimmed and chopped, 1 bay leaf, 12 black peppercorns, and 1 bouquet garni and cook over very low heat for about 15 minutes, or until the vegetables just begin to soften. Do not allow them to brown. Add 8 cups (2 qt/2 l) water and bring slowly to the boil. Reduce the heat, skim any scum from the surface, partly cover the saucepan, and cook on low heat for 2–3 hours. Strain the stock as for beef stock. Cool, then chill in the refrigerator overnight. Next day, carefully discard the solidified fat from the surface. Stock can be frozen for later use.

makes about 10 cups (2½ qt/2.5 l)

chicken stock Put 1 chicken, about 3 lb (1.5 kg), into a stockpot or large saucepan with 1 medium onion and 1 medium carrot, peeled and sliced, 1 rib (stick) celery, trimmed and chopped, 1 bouquet garni, 1 teaspoon black peppercorns and 8 cups (2 qt/2 l) water. Bring slowly to the boil. Proceed as for beef stock, simmering for 4–5 hours. Cool, then chill in the refrigerator overnight. Next day, carefully discard the solidified fat from the surface. Stock can be frozen for later use.

makes about 10 cups (2½ qt/2.5 l)

cooking and peeling chestnuts Using a small, sharp knife, cut a deep cross through the shell on the rounded side of each nut. Put the nuts into a saucepan and cover with cold water. Bring the water to the boil and boil the chestnuts on low heat for 5 minutes. Remove the saucepan from the heat and, using a slotted spoon, remove the nuts, three or four at a time, from the water. Peel off the shells—the fine inner brown skin should come away easily with the outer shell. Any stubborn pieces of inner skin that remain within the crevices of the nuts can be removed with tweezers. The nuts are easier to peel while warm. If necessary, bring the water back up to the boil. The peeled chestnuts are now ready for use as directed in recipes.

Roasted chestnuts are prepared in the same way, but are roasted for 20 minutes at 350°F (180°C/Gas Mark 4) instead of being boiled. Wrap them in a towel for a few minutes after they come out of the oven so you don't burn your fingers.

slow-cooked soups

pasta, lentil, and pepperoni soup

serves 6

1 cup (6½ oz/200 g) red lentils

4 cups (32 fl oz/1 liter) chicken stock, purchased or homemade

1 bay leaf

1 tablespoon olive oil

1 large onion, finely chopped

1 can (14 oz/440 g) tomatoes, undrained and roughly chopped

8 oz (250 g) small tube pasta or similar short pasta

6½ oz (200 g) pepperoni, thinly sliced

❖ Place the lentils, chicken stock, and bay leaf in a large saucepan and bring to the boil. Reduce the heat and simmer for 1–1¼ hours, or until the lentils are very soft. Purée the mixture in a food processor and return to the saucepan.

❖ Heat the oil in a frying pan on medium heat and cook the onion until soft, about 5 minutes. Add the onion and tomatoes to the saucepan containing the soup and simmer for 15 minutes.

❖ Cook the pasta in boiling salted water until al dente. Drain and stir into the soup together with the sliced pepperoni.

❖ When all the ingredients are well heated, serve immediately in warmed soup bowls.

split pea soup
with bacon

serves 4–6

Although the authentic version of this cool-weather favorite is smooth and creamy, you can give your split pea soup a little texture by setting aside some of the mixture before puréeing, then stirring the two batches together. Serve with fresh bread or with croutons fried in bacon fat or a little olive oil and garlic.

2 tablespoons olive oil

1 yellow onion, finely chopped

1 rib (stick) celery, thinly sliced

2 carrots, peeled and thinly sliced

1 clove garlic, chopped

1¼ cups (9 oz/280 g) green split peas, rinsed

6 slices (rashers) thick-cut bacon

7 cups (56 fl oz/1.75 l) water

1 bay leaf

¾ teaspoon salt

¼ teaspoon freshly ground pepper

1 tablespoon finely chopped fresh parsley

❖ Heat the oil in a large, heavy pot over medium heat and cook the onion for 3–5 minutes, or until softened. Add the celery and carrots and cook for 2–3 minutes longer, or until the carrots are tender. Add the garlic and cook for 1 minute longer.

❖ Add the split peas, bacon, water, and bay leaf, increase the heat to high, and bring just to the boil. Reduce the heat to medium–low and cook, partly covered, until the peas are soft, about 1 hour. Stir the soup occasionally during the cooking time and scrape the bottom of the pot to prevent scorching.

❖ Discard the bay leaf. Remove the bacon, cut it into small squares, and set aside.

❖ Using a blender, a food processor fitted with a metal blade, or a hand blender, purée the soup until smooth and creamy. If using a food processor or blender, return the purée to the pot.

❖ Reheat the soup over medium heat, stirring occasionally, until very hot. Season to taste with salt and pepper and stir in the reserved bacon. Ladle into warmed soup bowls and sprinkle the parsley over the top. Serve immediately.

chestnut and celery soup

serves 6–8

During the winter months, hot roasted chestnuts are often sold by vendors on the boulevards of Paris. The meaty nut is a popular ingredient in bistros around France, either fresh or as a canned purée. This rich soup, combining chestnut purée with celery, potato, and cream, is a popular first course for Christmas luncheons and New Year celebrations.

2 cups (1 lb/500 g) prepared unsweetened chestnut purée, or 1 1/2 lb (750 g) fresh chestnuts

1/2 cup (4 oz/125 g) unsalted butter

2 white onions, chopped

3 ribs (sticks) celery, coarsely chopped

1 large russet potato, peeled and coarsely chopped

6 cups (48 fl oz/1.5 l) chicken stock

2 cups (16 fl oz/500 ml) heavy (double) cream

1 tablespoon salt

1 teaspoon ground white pepper

❖ If you are using prepared chestnut purée, set aside. If you are using fresh chestnuts, preheat the oven to 400°F (200°C/Gas Mark 5). Using a sharp knife, cut an X on the flat side of each chestnut. Spread the chestnuts in a shallow pan and roast for 25–30 minutes, or until the nuts feel tender when pressed and the shells have curled back from the cuts. Remove from the oven and, using a small, sharp knife, remove the shells and the furry skin directly under them. (The nuts are easiest to peel when still warm. Put them back in the oven to warm again if they get too cool to peel easily.) Set aside.

❖ Melt the butter in a large saucepan over medium–high heat. Add the onions and celery and cook for about 5 minutes, or until golden brown.

❖ Add the chestnut purée or roasted chestnut flesh, potato, and chicken stock, stir well, and bring to a boil. Add the salt and white pepper, reduce the heat to medium–low, and simmer, uncovered, for about 1 hour, or until the soup thickens slightly.

❖ Working in batches, transfer the soup to a blender and process on high speed for about 1 minute, or until smooth and creamy.

❖ Return the soup to the saucepan, add the cream, and bring to a simmer over medium heat. Taste and adjust the seasoning, if necessary. Ladle into warmed bowls and serve immediately.

spicy lamb soup

serves 8

SPICE PASTE

1 piece fresh ginger, 1 inch (2.5 cm) long, peeled and coarsely chopped

6 cloves garlic, peeled

6 golden (French) shallots, about 1/2 lb (250 g), peeled and halved

1 1/2 teaspoons ground fennel

1 1/2 teaspoons ground cumin

1 tablespoon ground coriander

about 3 tablespoons water, or as needed

SOUP

1 1/2 lb (750 g) meaty lamb bones

12 cups (3 qt/3 l) water or meat stock (broth), purchased or homemade

2 tablespoons ghee or vegetable oil

2 leeks, including 1 inch (2.5 cm) of the tender green tops, rinsed and sliced

1 teaspoon curry powder

2 cardamom pods, bruised

2 whole star anise

1 cinnamon stick

4 whole cloves

1 large carrot, peeled and thickly sliced

2 teaspoons sugar

1 1/2 teaspoons salt

1 large tomato, cut into large wedges

fresh lime juice to taste (optional)

❖ To make the spice paste, process the ginger, garlic, shallots, fennel, cumin, and coriander to a smooth paste in a blender. Add the water as needed to facilitate blending. Set aside.

❖ To make the soup, preheat an oven to 450°F (220°C/Gas Mark 6).

❖ Remove all the meat from the lamb bones, cut into 1 inch (2.5 cm) cubes, and set aside. Place the bones in a roasting pan and roast, turning occasionally, for about 20 minutes, or until browned. Transfer the bones to a plate and set aside.

❖ Pour off the fat from the roasting pan and place the pan over medium heat. When the pan is hot, add 2 cups (16 fl oz/500 ml) of the water or stock and deglaze the pan by stirring to dislodge any browned bits from the pan bottom. Set aside.

❖ Melt the ghee or heat the vegetable oil in a large stockpot over medium heat. Add the leeks and cook for about 1 minute, or until golden.

❖ Add the spice paste and curry powder and cook for about 1 minute, or until fragrant. Add the roasted bones, reserved meat, the liquid from the roasting pan, and the remaining 10 cups (2½ qt/2.5 l) of water or stock.

❖ Wrap the cardamom, star anise, cinnamon, and cloves in a piece of cheesecloth (muslin), tie securely with kitchen string, and add to the pot. Bring to the boil, reduce the heat to low, and simmer, uncovered, for 30 minutes. Add the carrot and continue to simmer for about 30 minutes longer, or until the meat is tender. Season with the sugar and salt and stir in the tomato.

❖ Discard the cheesecloth-wrapped spices and the bones and ladle the soup into warmed bowls. Add lime juice to taste, if desired, and serve hot.

vegetarian white bean soup

Bean dishes are nourishing, satisfying, and economical, so they feature prominently in the cuisines of many countries. Serve this hearty soup in chunky pottery bowls with crusty country bread.

1 cup (7 oz/220 g) dried small white (navy) beans

¼ cup (2 fl oz/60 ml) vegetable oil

1 large yellow onion, finely chopped

1 clove garlic, finely chopped

1 large carrot, finely chopped

1 rib (stick) celery, finely chopped

5 cups (40 fl oz/1.25 l) vegetable stock (broth), purchased or homemade

1 can (1 lb/500 g) plum (Roma) tomatoes, with juice

1 teaspoon dried summer savory

1 teaspoon dried thyme

1 teaspoon sugar

1 bay leaf

salt and ground black pepper

2 tablespoons chopped fresh thyme

✧ Sort through the beans, discarding any grit or discolored beans. Put the beans in a bowl, add cold water to cover, and leave to soak for about 12 hours.

✧ Heat the oil in a large saucepan over medium heat. Add the onion, garlic, carrot, and celery and cook for 2–3 minutes, or until the onion is translucent.

✧ Drain the beans and add them to the saucepan along with the stock, tomatoes, savory, dried thyme, sugar, and bay leaf. Bring to the boil, reduce the heat to low, cover, and simmer, stirring occasionally to break up the tomatoes, for 2–2½ hours, or until the beans are very tender. Discard the bay leaf.

✧ Transfer about half of the soup to a food mill, a food processor fitted with a metal blade, or a blender. Purée, taking care to avoid splattering, and stir the purée back into the pan. Season to taste with salt and pepper. Ladle the soup into warmed bowls, garnish with the fresh thyme, and serve.

recipe variations

If you wish to make a non-vegetarian version of this soup, you can add a large chunk of ham or bacon, or two pork hocks, or four to six lamb shanks, or one chicken thigh for each person, or simply make the soup with chicken or meat stock (broth).

roasted eggplant soup
with mint

serves 4–6

Roasted eggplant develops
a rich, earthy, slightly smoky
flavor that is highlighted in
this simple soup.

For an edge of sweetness,
swirl some puréed roasted
red bell pepper (capsicum)
into each serving.

The soup can also be
served chilled.

1½ lb (750 g) small to medium
globe eggplant (aubergines)

2 tablespoons (1 oz/30 g) unsalted butter

1 small yellow onion, finely chopped

1 clove garlic, finely chopped

2½ cups (20 fl oz/625 ml) chicken or vegetable stock,
purchased or homemade

½ tablespoon finely chopped fresh mint

1 cup (8 fl oz/250 ml) heavy (double) cream

salt and ground white pepper

fresh mint sprigs

❖ Preheat the oven to 375°F (190°C/Gas Mark 4). Put the eggplant in a baking dish and puncture their skins several times with a fork. Roast in the oven, turning occasionally, for 1–1½ hours, or until the skins are evenly browned and deeply wrinkled. Let stand at room temperature until cool enough to handle, then peel.

❖ Melt the butter in a large saucepan over medium heat and cook the onion and garlic for 3–5 minutes, or until golden. Add the eggplant, breaking them up with a wooden spoon, and cook for 2–3 minutes more. Add the stock and mint and bring to the boil. Reduce the heat, cover, and simmer for about 20 minutes.

❖ Purée the soup, in small batches, in a food mill, a food processor fitted with a metal blade, or a blender, taking care to avoid splattering. Return the purée to the pan, stir in the cream, and gently heat through over low to medium heat. Season to taste with salt and white pepper. Ladle into warmed bowls, garnish with the mint sprigs, and serve.

recipe hint

The eggplant will have an even smokier flavor if they are grilled (barbecued) and the skins are allowed to blacken slightly.

When puréeing the soup, some people prefer to leave some of the texture, while others like to proceed until the soup is silky smooth.

serves 4–6

*½ cup (4 oz/125 g)
unsalted butter*

*4 large yellow onions,
thinly sliced*

salt

*5 cups (40 fl oz/1.25 l) beef
or veal stock*

2 bay leaves

freshly ground pepper

*8 oz (250 g) Gruyère or other
Swiss cheese, shredded*

*4–6 slices French bread,
½ inch (1 cm) thick,
toasted golden brown*

❖ Melt the butter in a large saucepan over low heat. Add the onions and sprinkle to taste with salt. Stir to coat well with the butter, cover, and cook, stirring occasionally, for 20–30 minutes, or until very tender. Remove the lid, increase the heat slightly, and cook, stirring frequently, for about 1 hour, or until the onions turn a deep caramel brown—take care not to let them burn.

❖ Add the stock and bay leaves, bring to the boil, reduce the heat, cover, and simmer for about 30 minutes more.

❖ Meanwhile, preheat the broiler (griller).

❖ Discard the bay leaves and season to taste with salt and pepper. Ladle the soup into heavy flameproof serving crocks or bowls and place on a baking sheet or broiler tray. Sprinkle a little of the cheese into each bowl, then place the toasted bread slices on top. Sprinkle evenly with the remaining cheese. Broil (grill) about 2 inches (5 cm) from the heat, for 2–3 minutes, or until the cheese is bubbly and golden. Serve immediately.

french onion soup
gratinée

minestrone

serves 6–8

¼ cup (2 fl oz/60 ml) olive oil

1 sweet onion, finely sliced

2 cloves garlic, finely chopped

2 slices (rashers) bacon, rind removed, finely diced

1 medium carrot, finely diced

2 ribs (sticks) celery, finely diced

8 cups (2 qt/2 l) beef or chicken stock

1 cup (8 fl oz/250 ml) canned or bottled chopped tomatoes

2 tablespoons tomato paste

2 cups (5 oz/150 g) finely shredded cabbage

4 oz (125 g) green beans, trimmed and cut into 1-inch (2.5-cm) pieces

2 oz (60 g) macaroni

salt and ground black pepper

10 oz (300 g) cooked or canned butter or kidney beans

⅓ cup (¾ oz/20 g) shredded basil leaves

grated Parmesan cheese, for sprinkling

❖ Heat the oil in a large frying pan. Cook the onion, garlic, bacon, carrot, and celery, stirring frequently, for 5 minutes, or until softened.

❖ Transfer to the slow cooker and pour on the stock. Add the chopped tomatoes and tomato paste. Put on the lid and cook on Low for 4–5 hours. Add the shredded cabbage, green beans, and macaroni during the final 2–3 hours of cooking.

❖ Season to taste with salt and black pepper. Stir through the butter or kidney beans. Serve in individual bowls sprinkled with shredded basil and grated Parmesan cheese.

27

2 tablespoons butter

6 green (spring) onions, finely chopped

2 ribs (sticks) celery, finely chopped

1 medium zucchini (courgette), finely diced

1 carrot, finely diced

8 cups (2 qt/2 l) chicken stock

2 medium potatoes, finely diced

1 large ripe tomato, seeded and chopped

2 chicken thigh fillets, trimmed of fat and finely diced

salt and ground black pepper

2 oz (60 g) green beans, diced

1/2 cup (2 3/4 oz/80 g) fresh or frozen peas

2 tablespoons chopped parsley

1/4 cup (1 3/4 oz/50 g) rice

snipped chives, to garnish

❖ Heat the butter in a large frying pan and cook the green onion, celery, zucchini, and carrot, stirring frequently, for 5 minutes, or until softened.

❖ Transfer to the slow cooker and pour on the stock. Add the diced potato, chopped tomato, and diced chicken meat. Season to taste with salt and pepper.

❖ Put on the lid and cook on Low for 8–10 hours. Add the green beans, peas, parsley, and rice during the final 3–4 hours of cooking.

❖ Garnish with chopped chives and serve hot, accompanied with fresh, crusty bread.

hearty chicken and vegetable soup

leek, onion,
and potato soup

serves 4–6

2 medium leeks

¼ cup (2 oz/60 g) butter

1 yellow onion,
finely chopped

3 medium potatoes,
peeled and diced

6 cups (1½ qt/1.5 l)
chicken or vegetable stock

½ cup (4 fl oz/125 ml)
sour cream

¼ cup (½ oz/15 g)
chopped parsley,
plus extra to garnish

salt and ground
black pepper

3 slices (rashers) bacon

❖ Trim the tops and roots from the leeks and discard the tough outer layer. Cut the leeks in half lengthwise and wash away any dirt under cold water. Drain, pat dry, and chop the leeks finely.

❖ Heat the butter in a large frying pan. Cook the leeks, onion, and potatoes, stirring frequently, for 4 minutes, or until softened a little. Transfer to the slow cooker and pour on the stock. Put on the lid and cook on Low for 4–5 hours, or on High for 2–3 hours.

❖ Combine the sour cream with a little of the liquid from the cooker. Stir into the soup together with the parsley. Season to taste with salt and pepper.

❖ While the soup is cooking, broil (grill) the bacon until crisp, drain on paper towels, then chop it. If desired, the cooked soup can be puréed roughly or until smooth.

❖ Serve the soup in warmed individual bowls, sprinkled with a little of the crumbled bacon and the extra parsley.

lamb and chickpea soup

serves 6–8

1¼ cups (8 oz/250 g) dried chickpeas
(garbanzo beans)

2 tablespoons olive oil

1½ lb (750 g) lamb shoulder

salt and ground black pepper

1 yellow onion, finely chopped

1 carrot, finely chopped

1 clove garlic, finely chopped

¾ teaspoon ground coriander

¾ teaspoon ground cumin

¼ teaspoon cayenne pepper

5 cups (40 fl oz/1.25 l) beef or chicken
stock, purchased or homemade

2 large plum (Roma) tomatoes, chopped

3 large lemons, cut into fourths

2 green (spring) onions, thinly sliced

4 tablespoons chopped fresh parsley

lamb and chickpea soup

❖ Sort through the chickpeas, discarding any grit or discolored peas. Put the chickpeas in a bowl, add cold water to cover, and leave to soak for about 12 hours.

❖ Heat the oil in a large pot over medium heat. Season the lamb with salt and pepper and fry for 3–4 minutes on each side, or until evenly browned. Remove the lamb and set aside. Pour off all but about 2 tablespoons of the fat.

❖ Add the onion, carrot, and garlic and cook over medium heat for 2–3 minutes, or until the onion is translucent. Add the coriander, cumin, and cayenne and cook for 1 minute more. Pour in the stock and deglaze the pot by stirring to dislodge any browned bits. Return the lamb to the pot.

❖ Drain the chickpeas and add them to the pot along with the tomatoes. Add 4 of the lemon wedges. Bring to the boil, reduce the heat to low, cover, and simmer, skimming regularly, for 2–2½ hours, or until the lamb and chickpeas are tender. Remove the lamb from the pot. Cut out and discard the bones and excess fat; cut the meat into small, coarse chunks and set aside. Discard the lemon wedges. Ladle about half of the chickpeas into a food mill, a food processor fitted with a metal blade, or a blender, and purée. Stir the purée and lamb chunks back into the pot.

❖ Gently reheat the soup. Ladle into warmed bowls and garnish with the green onions and parsley; pass the remaining lemon wedges separately.

macaroni and bean soup

1 cup (6½ oz/200 g) dried white (navy) beans,
soaked overnight in cold water and drained

4 oz (125 g) macaroni pasta

14 oz (400 g) speck, pancetta, or smoked bacon, cubed

2 large onions, chopped

1 clove garlic, finely chopped

4 large tomatoes, chopped

7 cups (56 fl oz/1.75 l) vegetable stock, purchased
or homemade

1 bouquet garni (see Glossary, page 310)

salt and ground black pepper

2 tablespoons chopped parsley, for garnish (optional)

❖ Combine all the ingredients, except the parsley, in a large saucepan and bring to the boil. Reduce the heat and simmer for 1–1½ hours, or until the beans are cooked through. Season to taste.

❖ Serve in warmed soup bowls and sprinkle with the chopped parsley, if desired.

cream of mushroom soup

serves 4–6

For a somewhat lighter soup, substitute 3 cups (24 fl oz/750 ml) chicken stock for 2 cups (16 fl oz/ 500 ml) of the cream and increase the simmering time by 5–10 minutes.

2 lb (1 kg) fresh mushrooms, wiped clean

¼ cup (2 fl oz/60 ml) vegetable oil

¼ cup (2 oz/60 g) unsalted butter

4 large green (spring) onions, finely chopped

2 tablespoons all-purpose (plain) flour

5 cups (40 fl oz/1.25 l) heavy (double) cream

pinch of ground nutmeg

salt and ground white pepper

2 tablespoons fresh lemon juice

1 tablespoon chopped chives

1 tablespoon finely chopped fresh parsley

✤ Set aside 4 attractive mushrooms and finely chop the remainder.

✤ Heat the oil and butter in a large saucepan over medium heat. Add the chopped mushrooms and green onions, increase the heat, and cook, stirring frequently, for 25–30 minutes, or until the vegetables have cooked down to a thick, dark brown paste. About halfway through the cooking time, when the mushroom liquid has evaporated, sprinkle in the flour and stir it in.

✤ Add the cream and deglaze the pan by stirring and scraping to dislodge any browned bits. Simmer, stirring occasionally, for 15–20 minutes more, or until thick.

✤ Purée the soup, in small batches, in a food mill, a food processor fitted with a metal blade, or a blender, taking care to avoid splattering. Return to the pan and heat gently, stirring in the nutmeg, and salt and white pepper to taste.

✤ Meanwhile, cut the reserved mushrooms into neat slices about ¼ inch (5 mm) thick. Toss them with the lemon juice in a small bowl.

✤ Ladle the soup into warmed bowls and garnish with the mushroom slices, chives, and parsley.

sausage and black bean soup

serves 6–8

3 cups (21 oz/655 g) dried black beans

1¾ lb (875 g) chorizo, andouille, or other spicy sausages

1 tablespoon olive oil

4 cloves garlic, finely chopped

2 yellow onions, finely chopped

2 ribs (sticks) celery, finely chopped

10 cups (2½ qt/2.5 l) chicken or meat stock, purchased or homemade

4 tablespoons chopped fresh parsley

1 teaspoon dried oregano

½ teaspoon ground cumin

2 bay leaves

½ tablespoon salt

½ cup (4 fl oz/125 ml) sour cream

2 tablespoons chopped chives

2 tablespoons chopped fresh cilantro (coriander)

◈ Sort through beans, discarding any grit or discolored beans. Set aside.

◈ Remove the casings from 1 lb (500 g) of the sausages. Heat the oil in a large saucepan on medium heat. Add the sausage meat and cook, coarsely breaking up the meat with a wooden spoon, for about 5 minutes, or until lightly browned. Pour off all but about 3 tablespoons of the fat. Return the pan to the heat, add the garlic, onions, and celery, and cook for 2–3 minutes, or until the onions are translucent.

◈ Add the beans, stock, parsley, oregano, cumin, and bay leaves and bring to the boil. Reduce the heat, cover, and simmer for 2–2½ hours, or until the beans are very tender. Halfway through the cooking time, add half the salt and a little water, if necessary, to keep the beans moist.

◈ Discard the bay leaves. Purée a few ladlefuls of beans in a food mill, a food processor fitted with a metal blade, or a blender, taking care to avoid splattering. Stir back into the pan with the remaining salt. Taste and adjust the seasoning.

◈ Cut the remaining sausages into slices about ½ inch (1 cm) thick. Cook in a nonstick frying pan over medium heat for about 3 minutes per side, or until browned. Ladle the soup into warmed bowls; garnish with sour cream, sausage slices, chives, and cilantro.

spicy seven-bean soup

serves 6–8

1/4 cup (11/4 oz/45 g) each dried baby lima beans, black-eyed peas, chickpeas (garbanzo beans), kidney beans, small white (navy) beans, pinto beans, and red beans

1 green or red bell pepper (capsicum)

1/4 cup (2 fl oz/60 ml) olive oil

2 cloves garlic, finely chopped

1 large fresh, mild, green chile, finely chopped

1 yellow onion, finely chopped

1 carrot, finely chopped

1 rib (stick) celery, finely chopped

1 teaspoon crushed dried chile

4 cups (32 fl oz/1 liter) chicken or vegetable stock, purchased or homemade

1 can (1 lb/500 g) crushed tomatoes

2 tablespoons tomato paste

1 tablespoon sugar

1 tablespoon dried basil

1 tablespoon dried oregano

1 tablespoon red wine vinegar

2 teaspoons dried thyme

2 bay leaves

salt and ground black pepper

1/2 cup (1/2 oz/15 g) chopped fresh parsley

✧ Sort through the beans, discarding any grit or discolored beans. Put the beans in a bowl, add cold water to cover, and leave to soak for about 12 hours.

✧ Discard the seeds and ribs of the bell pepper and dice the flesh. Heat the oil in a large pot over medium heat. Add the garlic, bell pepper, chile, onion, carrot, celery, and dried chile. Cook for 2–3 minutes, or until the onion is translucent.

✧ Drain the beans and stir them into the pot along with the stock, tomatoes, tomato paste, sugar, basil, oregano, vinegar, thyme, and bay leaves. Bring to the boil, reduce the heat to low, and simmer, partly covered, for 2–2½ hours, or until the beans are tender.

✧ Just before serving, discard the bay leaves. Season to taste with salt and pepper, and stir in the parsley.

recipe variation

You can mix the beans in any combination or variety you wish—just measure the same total quantity of them.

cabbage soup
with flank steak

serves 8–10

You can substitute kielbasa sausages or other sausages for the flank steak; just cut into slices ½ inch (1 cm) thick and add to the pot with the cabbage.

¼ cup (2 fl oz/60 ml) vegetable oil

1 large yellow onion, coarsely chopped

2 cloves garlic, coarsely chopped

1 lb (500 g) flank steak, trimmed of fat

salt and ground black pepper

8 cups (2 qt/2 l) meat stock, purchased or homemade, or water

1 can (1 lb/500 g) plum (Roma) tomatoes, with juice

⅓ cup (2½ fl oz/80 ml) fresh lemon juice

¼ cup (2 oz/60 g) sugar

¼ cup (1 oz/30 g) raisins, golden or dark

1 head Savoy cabbage, cored and cut into shreds about ½ inch (1 cm) wide

2 bay leaves

❖ Heat the oil in a large pot on low to medium heat. Add the onion and garlic and cook for 2–3 minutes, or until translucent. Lightly season the flank steak with salt and pepper, add to the pan, and cook, turning once, for 2–3 minutes, or until lightly browned on each side.

❖ Add the stock and deglaze the pan by stirring and scraping to dislodge any browned bits.

❖ Add the tomatoes, crushing them slightly with a wooden spoon. Add the lemon juice, sugar, raisins, cabbage, and bay leaves. Increase the heat and bring to the boil. Reduce the heat to low, partly cover, and simmer for about 1 hour, or until the meat is tender.

❖ Discard the bay leaves. Remove the meat from the pot and, using a sharp knife and a fork, cut and tear it up into coarse, bite-size shreds. Stir the meat back into the pot. Taste the soup and adjust the seasoning, if necessary. Ladle the soup into warmed bowls and serve.

recipe hint

The flavors in this hearty soup meld and develop so that it tastes even better if you make it the day before serving and chill it in the refrigerator—do not freeze. Reheat it gently, just before you are ready to dish up, and serve it with crusty country bread.

hearty chicken soup with dumplings

serves 6

1/2 cup (4 oz/125 g) pearl barley

1/2 lb (250 g) frozen lima (broad) beans

2 tablespoons oil

2 lb (1 kg) boneless, skinless chicken breasts, sliced

3 leeks, well-washed, trimmed, and sliced

2 cloves garlic, crushed

3 ribs (sticks) celery, chopped

3 medium carrots, chopped

2 medium zucchini (courgettes), chopped

8 cups (2 qt/2 l) chicken stock, purchased or homemade

1/2 cup tomato paste

1/4 cup (1/2 oz/15 g) chopped fresh parsley

1 tablespoon chopped fresh thyme

salt and ground black pepper

DUMPLINGS

1/4 cup (1 1/2 oz/45 g) cornmeal (polenta)

3/4 cup (3 1/2 oz/100 g) all-purpose (plain) flour

1 1/2 teaspoons baking powder

1/4 teaspoon salt

1/2 cup grated Parmesan cheese

1/4 cup (2 oz/60 g) cold butter, grated

about 1/2 cup (4 fl oz/125 ml) water

◈ Rinse the barley under cold running water until the water runs clear; drain.

◈ Pour boiling water over the beans, drain, and slip off the loosened skins.

◈ Heat the oil in a large saucepan, and cook the chicken in batches until well browned all over—this is important to achieve the best color and flavor. Add the leeks, garlic, celery, carrots, and zucchini, and cook, stirring, until the leeks are soft. Add the chicken stock and tomato paste, and bring to the boil. Add the barley and simmer, covered, for 20 minutes. Return the chicken to the pan and add the beans.

◈ To make the dumplings, combine the dry ingredients in a bowl, stir in the cheese and butter, and mix well. Add enough of the water to form a soft dough. Drop level tablespoons of dumpling mixture into the simmering soup, cover, and simmer for about 15 minutes, or until the dumplings are cooked through and the barley is tender. Do not lift the lid for at least 10 minutes after adding the dumplings or they will become stodgy.

◈ Stir in the herbs, season to taste with salt and pepper, and serve immediately.

provençal garlic soup

serves 4–6

Despite the prodigious amount of garlic in this recipe, the resulting soup is surprisingly mellow.

Always trim any green shoots from the garlic cloves, as they carry the sharp flavor.

In spring, borage blossoms make a lovely garnish.

8 cups (2 qt/2 l) water

¾ cup (3 oz/100 g) garlic cloves

¼ cup (2 fl oz/60 ml) olive oil

½ cup (2 oz/60 g) sliced white onion

⅓ cup (1½ oz/45 g) sliced celery

⅓ cup (1½ oz/45 g) sliced fennel

½ cup (4 fl oz/125 ml) dry white wine

4 fresh thyme sprigs

½ teaspoon fresh rosemary leaves

1 bay leaf

5 cups (40 fl oz/1.25 l) chicken stock

2¼ cups (18 fl oz/560 ml) heavy (double) cream

1 slice coarse country-style bread, preferably a day old, roughly chopped

1 tablespoon salt

1 teaspoon ground white pepper

❖ Bring the water and garlic cloves to the boil in a large saucepan over high heat. Reduce the heat to medium and simmer, uncovered, for about 5 minutes, or until the garlic is translucent. Drain and reserve the garlic.

❖ Return the saucepan to medium heat and heat the olive oil for 30 seconds. Add the onion, celery, and fennel and cook for 2–3 minutes, or until just tender. Add the garlic cloves, reduce the heat slightly, and cook, stirring frequently, for another 2 minutes. Do not allow to brown. Add the white wine and cook until reduced by half.

❖ Add the thyme, rosemary, bay leaf, chicken stock, cream, bread, and salt and pepper to taste. Stir well, reduce the heat to low, and simmer, uncovered, stirring occasionally, for about 40 minutes, or until creamy white and reduced by one fourth. Remove from the heat and cool for 10 minutes.

❖ Working in two batches, transfer the soup to a blender and blend until smooth. Return to the saucepan.

❖ Reheat over medium heat. Serve immediately in warmed individual bowls.

slow-cooked
main
dishes

beef in the pot

serves 6

4 lb (2 kg) boneless beef roast
(rump, chuck, or topside)

1 tablespoon vegetable oil

½ cup (4 fl oz/125 ml) red wine

½ cup (4 fl oz/125 ml)
tomato purée

1 tablespoon Worcestershire
sauce

1 clove garlic, crushed

salt and ground black pepper

6 whole baby carrots

1 yellow onion,
cut into wedges

6 small new potatoes

1 tablespoon cornstarch
(cornflour) (optional)

❖ Pat the meat dry with paper towels. Heat the oil in a large frying pan and brown the meat well on all sides. Place the meat in the slow cooker. Deglaze the frying pan with the red wine. Add the tomato purée, Worcestershire sauce, and garlic, and pour the mixture onto the meat. Season with salt and pepper.

❖ Surround the meat with the carrots, onion, and potatoes. Put on the lid and cook on Low for 10–12 hours, or High for 6–8 hours. Serve the beef sliced with a little of the sauce and the vegetables.

❖ To thicken the beef juices, if desired, mix the cornstarch to a smooth paste with a little water. Add to the beef juices and stir until thickened.

lamb shoulder
with garlic and thyme

serves 4

The combination of lamb with garlic and herbs is a classic European favorite. To vary the recipe, serve it with a range of different side dishes, such as spicy couscous with chickpeas (garbanzo beans), ratatouille, or an Italian vegetable casserole.

3 tablespoons olive oil

2 lb (1 kg) boneless lamb shoulder, trimmed of fat and cut into 1-inch (2.5-cm) cubes

½ cup (2½ oz/75 g) chopped white onion

1 small carrot, peeled and diced

1 head garlic, separated into cloves and peeled

salt and ground black pepper

1 tomato, coarsely chopped

1 tablespoon finely chopped fresh thyme

1 cup (8 fl oz/250 ml) dry white wine

3 cups (24 fl oz/750 ml) veal or beef stock

❖ Heat 2 tablespoons of the olive oil in a large frying pan over high heat. Working in batches, add the lamb and cook for about 5 minutes, or until the meat begins to brown. Using a slotted spoon, transfer the meat to a plate and set aside.

❖ Pour off the fat from the pan and place over medium–high heat. Add the remaining oil and cook the onion, carrot, and garlic for 4–5 minutes, or until the vegetables begin to brown.

❖ Return the lamb to the pan and add 1 teaspoon salt, ¼ teaspoon pepper, the tomato, thyme, and wine. Reduce the heat to medium and cook for about 5 minutes, or until the liquid is reduced by half. Add the veal stock and bring to the boil over high heat. Reduce the heat to medium and simmer for about 45 minutes, or until the lamb is tender when pierced with a fork.

❖ Pour the contents of the frying pan through a fine-mesh sieve into a clean container. Remove the meat from the sieve and keep it warm.

❖ Place the vegetables and all of the strained liquid into a food processor fitted with a metal blade, or a blender, and process or blend on high speed for about 30 seconds, or until the sauce is smooth.

❖ Pour the sauce into a saucepan and reheat over medium heat. Adjust the seasoning to taste, if necessary, with salt and pepper. Divide the lamb among warmed serving plates and pour a little sauce over. Pass any extra sauce separately.

veal casserole

serves 4

12 oz (375 g) pearl onions

1½ lb (750 g) boneless veal
shoulder, cut into 1-inch
(2.5-cm) cubes

¼ cup (1½ oz/45 g) all-purpose
(plain) flour

2 tablespoons olive oil

2 oz (60 g) green (spring)
onion, roughly chopped

1 cup (8 fl oz/250 ml)
white wine

1 teaspoon dried
tarragon leaves

8 oz (250 g) button mushrooms

salt and ground black pepper

½ cup (½ oz/15 g)
chopped parsley

❧ Trim the roots from the pearl onions. Place the onions in a saucepan of boiling water and boil for 2 minutes. Drain, cool, and remove the skins.

❧ Pat the meat cubes dry with paper towels then dust the veal with the flour. Heat half the oil in a large frying pan and fry the veal in 2–3 batches over high heat, adding the remaining oil as needed. Transfer the meat to the slow cooker.

❧ Add the pearl onions, green onion, white wine, and tarragon leaves to the frying pan. Cook, stirring, for 2–3 minutes, or until the wine has evaporated a little. Add to the veal in the slow cooker. Stir in the mushrooms and season well with salt and pepper.

❧ Put on the lid and cook on Low for 8–10 hours, or High for 5–6 hours. Stir, sprinkle with parsley, and serve.

pork chops
and apple in cider

serves 4

4 pork loin chops

2 tablespoons all-purpose
(plain) flour, plus
1 tablespoon extra

2 tablespoons (1 oz/30 g) butter

1 tablespoon oil

2 sweet onions, thinly sliced

1 rib (stick) celery, sliced

2 apples, peeled,
cored, and cut into fourths

2 sprigs fresh thyme

salt and ground black pepper

1 cup (8 fl oz/250 ml)
apple cider

❖ Trim any excess fat from the pork chops. Dust with the 2 tablespoons flour, shaking off the excess. Heat the butter and oil in a large frying pan and cook the onions and celery for 3–4 minutes, or until softened. Using a slotted spoon, transfer to the slow cooker.

❖ Increase the heat, add the pork chops to the frying pan, and cook on both sides until lightly golden. Place the chops in the slow cooker, add the apple wedges and thyme sprigs, and season with salt and pepper.

❖ Mix the extra flour to a smooth paste in a small bowl with a little of the cider, add the remaining cider, and pour over the pork chops in the slow cooker.

❖ Put on the lid and cook on Low for 6–8 hours. Remove the thyme sprigs and skim any fat from the surface. Serve hot with buttered noodles.

beef rendang

serves 4

1 oz (30 g) tamarind pulp

½ cup (4 fl oz/125 ml) boiling water

SPICE PASTE

1 teaspoon coriander seeds

1 teaspoon cumin seeds

10 dried small red chiles, seeded, soaked in
lukewarm water for 15 minutes, and drained

2 stalks lemongrass, tender white heart
section only, chopped, or zest of 1 lemon

3 fresh galangal slices, each 1 inch (2.5 cm)
in diameter, chopped; or 1½ dried galangal
slices, soaked in warm water to soften,
drained, and chopped

1 piece fresh ginger, 1 inch (2.5 cm) long,
peeled and chopped

2 cloves garlic

3 green (spring) onions

about 3 tablespoons water

3 tablespoons unsweetened shredded
dried coconut

3 tablespoons vegetable oil

2 cinnamon sticks

2 cardamom pods

4 whole star anise

2½ lb (1.25 kg) boneless beef chuck,
round, or stewing meat, cut into 1½-inch
(4-cm) cubes

1 can (14 fl oz/440 ml) coconut milk

4 kaffir lime leaves

2 teaspoons sugar

½ teaspoon salt

❖ Soak the tamarind pulp in the boiling water in a small bowl for 15 minutes. Mash with the back of a fork to help disperse the pulp. Pour through a fine-mesh sieve into another small bowl, pressing against the pulp to extract as much flavorful liquid as possible. Discard the pulp and set the liquid aside.

❖ For the spice paste, toast the coriander and cumin seeds in a small, dry frying pan over medium heat for 2–3 minutes, or until fragrant. Let cool, then transfer to a spice grinder or mortar. Grind or pulverize with a pestle until finely ground. Transfer to a blender or mini food processor and add the rehydrated chiles, lemongrass or lemon zest, galangal, ginger, garlic, green onions, and 3 tablespoons water. Blend to a smooth paste, adding more water if needed.

❖ Toast the coconut in a small, dry frying pan over medium heat for 1–2 minutes, or until golden brown. When cool, transfer to a spice grinder or mortar. Grind or mash with a pestle as finely as possible.

❖ Heat the oil in a wok over medium heat, add the spice paste, and fry gently, stirring continuously, for 5–8 minutes, or until fragrant, thick, and creamy. Add the cinnamon sticks, cardamom pods, star anise, ground coconut, tamarind liquid, and beef. Cook, turning often to coat the beef thoroughly with the spice paste, for about 3 minutes. Add the coconut milk and bring to the boil. Reduce the heat to medium and simmer, uncovered, for about 45 minutes, or until the beef is tender.

❖ Cut the lime leaves into fine slivers and add to the pot along with the sugar and salt. Continue to simmer, stirring occasionally, for about 20 minutes longer, or until the sauce has reduced, is no longer milky, and coats the fork-tender meat with a thin film of oil. Serve hot.

osso buco
with gremolata

serves 4

4 thick slices veal shin (osso buco)

2 tablespoons all-purpose (plain) flour

2 tablespoons butter

2 tablespoons olive oil

1 medium yellow onion, finely chopped

4 cloves garlic, finely chopped

1 carrot, diced

½ cup (4 fl oz/125 ml) white wine

4 ripe tomatoes, peeled, seeded,
and chopped

1 tablespoon tomato paste

salt and ground black pepper

GREMOLATA

2 cloves garlic, finely chopped

1 cup (1 oz/30 g) finely chopped parsley

finely grated zest of 1 lemon

✥ Pat the veal dry with paper towels then dust with the flour. Heat half the butter and half the oil in a large frying pan. Fry the veal over high heat until browned on both sides. Transfer to the slow cooker.

✥ Heat the remaining butter and oil in the frying pan. Add the onion, garlic, and carrot. Cook, stirring, for 2 minutes then add the white wine. Cook, stirring, for 2–3 minutes, or until the wine has evaporated a little. Stir in the chopped tomatoes and tomato paste and pour over the veal in the slow cooker. Season well with salt and pepper. Put on the lid and cook on Low for 8–10 hours, or High for 5–6 hours.

✥ For the gremolata, combine all the ingredients in a small bowl.

✥ To serve, arrange the osso buco on warmed plates and sprinkle with gremolata. Serve with Mashed Potatoes (page 66).

recipe hint

Gremolata is the classic Italian accompaniment for osso buco, but it is also good sprinkled over other veal dishes, or with baked fish, or artichokes.

When buying veal for osso buco, choose cuts from the shin of the hind leg, which is meatier than the foreleg.

chicken
provençal

serves 4

1 chicken, 3 lb (1.5 kg), cut into 8 pieces

1/3 cup (2 oz/60 g) all-purpose (plain) flour

2 tablespoons olive oil

2 tablespoons butter

1 sweet onion, roughly chopped

4 cloves garlic, chopped

1 small red bell pepper (capsicum), seeded and thickly sliced

1 small yellow bell pepper (capsicum), seeded and thickly sliced

2 large ripe tomatoes, peeled, seeded, and roughly chopped

2 tablespoons tomato paste or purée

2 oil-packed anchovies, chopped

1 cup (8 fl oz/250 ml) chicken stock

2 small zucchini (courgettes), thickly sliced

1/2 cup (2 oz/60 g) black olives

1/2 cup (2 oz/60 g) green olives

1/2 cup (1/2 oz/15 g) chopped parsley

❖ Pat the chicken pieces dry with paper towels. Place the flour in a plastic bag, add the chicken pieces, and shake to coat evenly with flour.

❖ Heat half the oil and half the butter in a large frying pan and cook the chicken pieces, in 2 batches, adding the remaining butter and oil as needed. Cook, turning, for 3–4 minutes, or until the chicken pieces are golden brown. Place in the slow cooker.

❖ Add the onion, garlic, and bell peppers to the pan and cook, stirring, for 2–3 minutes. Add the tomatoes, tomato paste or purée, anchovies, and stock. Stir in the zucchini.

❖ Add the contents of the frying pan to the slow cooker. Put on the lid and cook on Low for 7–9 hours. Stir in the olives and parsley. Serve hot with Mashed Potatoes (page 66) or plain cooked pasta.

recipe variations

There are many regional variations of this simple chicken and vegetable casserole. If you substitute cider, cream, and apples for the tomatoes, anchovies, and olives, for example, you will have a dish that would be quite at home on a dinner table in Normandy.

pork ragout
with red bell peppers

serves 4–6

This recipe combines the best of two classic Portuguese dishes. One browns and then braises pork slices with sweet red bell peppers and white wine; the other stews cumin-and-garlic-scented pork in white wine. The aromatic result is perfectly accented with slices of lemon and chopped cilantro (fresh coriander).

3 tablespoons cumin seeds

2 tablespoons chopped garlic

1 teaspoon coarse salt or sea salt

1 teaspoon ground pepper

1 tablespoon paprika

2 lb (1 kg) boneless pork shoulder

¼ cup (2 oz/60 g) lard
or ¼ cup (2 fl oz/60 ml) olive oil

4 red bell peppers (capsicums), seeds and ribs removed, cut lengthwise into strips ½ inch (1 cm) wide

1 cup (8 fl oz/250 ml) dry white wine

½ cup (4 fl oz/125 ml) chicken stock

6 paper-thin lemon slices, cut into half rounds

½ cup (¾ oz/20 g) chopped fresh cilantro (coriander)

✥ Toast the cumin seeds in a small, dry frying pan over medium heat, swirling the pan occasionally, for 2–3 minutes, or until fragrant. Transfer to a spice grinder or peppermill and grind finely. Combine the ground cumin, garlic, salt, pepper, and paprika, and mash in a mortar with a pestle to form a paste.

✥ Cut the pork into 1-inch (2.5-cm) cubes. Place in a nonreactive bowl and rub the paste evenly over the meat. Cover and let marinate overnight in the refrigerator.

✥ Bring the meat to room temperature. Heat the lard or oil in a large frying pan over high heat and, working in batches, cook the pork for 5–8 minutes, or until browned on all sides. Using tongs or a slotted spoon, transfer the pork to a large, heavy pot. Add the bell pepper strips to the fat remaining in the pan and cook for about 5 minutes, or until softened.

✥ Transfer the bell pepper strips to the pot containing the pork. Return the frying pan to high heat, add the wine, and deglaze the pan by stirring to dislodge any browned bits from the bottom of the pan. Add the pan juices to the pork and bell peppers. Add the stock and lemon slices and bring to the boil. Quickly reduce the heat to low, cover, and simmer for about 25 minutes, or until the pork is very tender.

✥ Stir in the cilantro, then taste and adjust the seasoning, if necessary. Spoon into a warmed serving dish and serve hot.

pork and sweet potato stew

serves 6

3 tablespoons olive oil

1 red (Spanish) onion, cut into
thin wedges

2 lb (1 kg) lean pork tenderloin or
steak, cut into 1-inch (2.5-cm) cubes

1/2 cup (4 fl oz/125 ml)
white wine or sherry

12 oz (375 g) sweet potato, peeled
and cut into 1 1/2-inch (4-cm) cubes

1/2 cup (4 fl oz/125 ml) chicken
stock or water

2 tablespoons maple syrup

salt and ground black pepper

1/2 cup (1/2 oz/15 g) chopped parsley

❖ Heat 1 tablespoon of the oil in a large frying
pan and cook the onion for 2–3 minutes. Transfer
to the slow cooker with a slotted spoon.

❖ Pat the pork cubes dry with paper towels. Cook
the pork over high heat in 2 or 3 batches, adding
the remaining oil as necessary. Transfer to the slow
cooker with a slotted spoon.

❖ Deglaze the pan with the wine or sherry,
stirring to dislodge any browned bits from the
bottom of the pan. Pour over the pork. Add the
sweet potato cubes, stock, and maple syrup.
Season to taste with salt and pepper.

❖ Put on the lid and cook on Low for 7–9 hours.
Stir in the parsley and serve hot with pasta.

chicken
marengo

8 chicken pieces, about 3 lb (1.5 kg)

⅓ cup (2 oz/60 g) all-purpose (plain) flour

2 tablespoons olive oil

2 tablespoons butter

6 green (spring) onions, including the green tops, thickly sliced

2 cloves garlic, finely chopped

2 tablespoons brandy

1 cup (8 fl oz/250 ml) chicken stock

2 large ripe tomatoes, peeled and roughly chopped

12 medium mushrooms, thickly sliced

2 sprigs fresh oregano

salt and ground black pepper

fresh oregano leaves, to garnish

◈ Pat the chicken pieces dry with paper towels. Place the flour in a plastic bag, add the chicken, and shake to coat evenly with flour.

◈ Heat half the oil and half the butter in a large frying pan and cook the chicken, in 2 batches, adding the remaining butter and oil as necessary. Cook, turning, for 3–4 minutes, or until golden brown. Place in the slow cooker.

◈ Add the spring onions and garlic to the frying pan and cook for 1–2 minutes. Pour in the brandy and stock, and bring to the boil. Pour over the chicken pieces then add the tomatoes, mushrooms, and oregano sprigs. Season to taste with salt and pepper. Put on the lid and cook on Low for 7–9 hours, or High for 4–5 hours. Remove oregano sprigs and sprinkle with the oregano leaves. Serve hot with rice.

roast turkey
with mashed potatoes
and gravy

serves 6

¼ cup (2 fl oz/60 ml) olive oil

1 clove garlic, chopped

1 teaspoon dried thyme, crumbled

1 teaspoon dried sage, crumbled

ground black pepper

1 boneless turkey breast, about 3¼ lb (1.6 kg), rolled and tied

salt

2 cups (16 fl oz/500 ml) chicken stock

GRAVY

½ cup (4 fl oz/125 ml) water

2 tablespoons unsalted butter

2 tablespoons all-purpose (plain) flour

1 cup (8 fl oz/250 ml) chicken stock, warmed

salt and ground black pepper

Mashed Potatoes (page 66), to serve

❖ Combine the olive oil, garlic, thyme, sage, and ⅛ teaspoon pepper in a large baking dish. Place the turkey breast in the dish and rub the mixture over the entire surface. Cover and refrigerate overnight, basting a few times with the marinade.

❖ Preheat the oven to 350°F (180°C/Gas Mark 4).

❖ Place the breast on a rack in a roasting pan, season lightly with salt and pepper, and pour half of the chicken stock over the breast and into the bottom of the pan. Roast, basting with the pan juices every 5–10 minutes, for about 1 hour and 20 minutes, or until an instant-read thermometer inserted into the center registers 165°F (74°C). Check the pan periodically during roasting and add the remaining stock to the pan as it becomes dry. Transfer the breast to a warmed serving platter and cover with aluminum foil to rest while you make the gravy.

❖ To make the gravy, place the roasting pan on the stove top over high heat, add the water, and deglaze the pan by stirring to dislodge any browned bits on the bottom of the pan. Boil for about 2 minutes, or until the liquid is reduced by half. Remove from the heat and set aside.

❖ Melt the butter in a saucepan over medium heat. Sprinkle the flour over the butter and whisk constantly for 2–3 minutes, or until the flour is absorbed and the mixture is bubbling and golden. Add the reduced pan drippings and warmed chicken stock and continue to whisk for 7–10 minutes, or until thickened. Season to taste with salt and pepper.

❖ Snip and discard the string from the turkey breast. Slice the meat and serve on warmed individual plates with a mound of mashed potatoes. Drizzle the gravy over the turkey and potatoes, or pass separately in a warmed pitcher.

roast turkey with mashed potatoes and gravy

mashed potatoes

serves 6

*3 lb (1.5 kg) white, red, yellow-fleshed, or boiling potatoes, peeled and cut
into 2-inch (5-cm) pieces*

1½ teaspoons salt, plus extra to taste

⅓ cup (2½ oz/75 g) unsalted butter, cut into small pieces

1 cup (8 fl oz/250 ml) plus 2 tablespoons half-and-half (half cream), heated

ground white pepper

❖ Cover the potato pieces with water in a large bowl and let stand for 5 minutes to remove
the excess starch. Drain. Bring a large saucepan three-fourths full of water to the boil. Add
1½ teaspoons salt and the potatoes and return to the boil. Boil for about 15 minutes, or until
the potatoes are tender when pierced with a fork. Drain well and return to the empty pan.

❖ Place the pan over high heat and, tossing the potatoes to prevent scorching, heat for
1–2 minutes to dry the potatoes. Remove from the heat. Mash the potatoes with a potato
masher until they are almost smooth. Add the butter, mash together, and then add the
half-and-half, a little at a time, stirring with a spoon when the potatoes are smooth. The
potatoes should be creamy but not soupy.

❖ Season to taste with salt and white pepper, transfer to a warmed serving dish, and
serve immediately.

grilled butterflied leg of lamb with couscous

serves 6–8

1 leg of lamb, about 5 lb (2.5 kg),
boned and butterflied
(about 4 lb/2 kg boned)

¼ cup (2 fl oz/60 ml) extra-virgin
olive oil

1 tablespoon chopped garlic

2 teaspoons salt

2 teaspoons cracked pepper

1½ teaspoons chopped fresh rosemary

grated zest and juice of 1 lemon

COUSCOUS

4 cups (1½ lb/750 g) couscous
(see Glossary, page 311)

4 cups (32 fl oz/1 liter) chicken stock
or water

1 red bell pepper (capsicum), seeded
and diced

1 teaspoon saffron threads

1 teaspoon chopped garlic

1 teaspoon salt

½ cup (1 oz/30 g) chopped green
(spring) onions

½ cup (2 oz/60 g) dried currants

¼ cup (1½ oz/45 g) pine nuts, toasted
(see Glossary, page 312)

1 tablespoon chopped fresh mint

2 tablespoons extra-virgin olive oil

fresh mint sprigs, to garnish

grilled butterflied leg of lamb with couscous

❖ Place the leg of lamb in a nonmetallic dish. Combine the olive oil in a small shallow bowl with the garlic, salt, pepper, rosemary, lemon zest, and lemon juice. Drizzle the mixture over the lamb, and rub it in well. Cover and refrigerate for at least 3 hours, or for as long as overnight. About 1 hour before cooking, remove the lamb from the refrigerator and bring to room temperature.

❖ Prepare a fire in a charcoal grill (barbecue) using hardwood charcoal, such as mesquite or hickory. When the coals have burned down to a gray ash, place the lamb on the grill rack with the skin side down. Grill (barbecue) for about 10 minutes. Turn over and grill for about 10 minutes longer for medium-rare. Transfer to a large platter to rest for 5 minutes.

❖ Meanwhile, place the couscous in a heatproof bowl. Heat the chicken stock in a small saucepan over high heat with the bell pepper, saffron, garlic, and salt until boiling. Pour over the couscous, stir to combine, then cover with plastic wrap or aluminum foil. Let stand for 8 minutes. Using a fork, fluff the couscous to break it into individual grains. Let rest for 5 minutes longer. Add the green onions, currants, pine nuts, mint, and olive oil, and toss well to combine.

❖ Serve the couscous at room temperature or briefly reheat in a large nonstick frying pan over high heat, tossing often, for 1–2 minutes. Thinly slice the lamb across the grain and arrange on individual plates along with a mound of couscous. Garnish with a mint sprig and serve.

salsa chicken and rice

serves 4–6

6 boneless, skinless chicken breast halves (about 1½ lb/750 g total weight)

2 tablespoons vegetable oil

1 medium yellow onion, chopped

½ green bell pepper (capsicum), seeded and chopped

2 cloves garlic, finely chopped

1 teaspoon ground cumin

1 teaspoon dried ground oregano

1 cup (6½ oz/200 g) long-grain rice

2 cups (16 fl oz/500 ml) chicken stock

1 cup (8 fl oz/250 ml) purchased chunky salsa

salt and ground black pepper

1 cup (5 oz/155 g) fresh or frozen peas

⅓ cup (¾ oz/20 g) chopped fresh cilantro (coriander)

❖ Cut the chicken breasts into large pieces. Pat dry with paper towels. Heat half the oil in a large frying pan on high heat and brown the chicken on all sides. Place in the slow cooker.

❖ Heat the remaining oil in the frying pan and cook the onion, bell pepper, and garlic, stirring, for 2–3 minutes. Stir in the cumin, oregano, rice, stock, and salsa. Bring to the boil then pour over the chicken in the slow cooker. Add salt and pepper to taste.

❖ Put on the lid and cook on Low for 3–4 hours. Half an hour before serving, stir in the peas and cilantro. Serve hot.

pork spareribs
with redcurrant sauce

serves 4

*1 large onion,
finely chopped*

2 cloves garlic, crushed

*¾ cup (8 oz/250 g)
redcurrant jelly*

*¼ cup (3 fl oz/100 ml)
honey*

*¼ cup (2 fl oz/60 ml)
soy sauce*

*¼ cup (2 fl oz/60 ml)
white wine vinegar*

*½–1 teaspoon hot
chile sauce*

ground black pepper

*2 lb (1 kg) pork
spareribs*

❖ Combine the onion, garlic, jelly, honey, soy sauce, vinegar, chile sauce to taste, and pepper in a bowl. Add the spareribs and stir well to coat with the marinade. Cover and refrigerate overnight, or for at least 30 minutes, so the pork can absorb the flavors of the marinade.

❖ Preheat the oven to 425°F (210°C/ Gas Mark 5). Reserving the marinade, remove the spareribs and place in a single layer in a roasting pan. Bake for 30 minutes. Reduce the heat to 375°F (190°C/Gas Mark 4). Pour off the excess fat, spoon on the marinade, and bake, turning the ribs occasionally and basting with the marinade, for 1 hour more (the sauce can be thinned, as necessary, during the cooking time with stock or orange juice).

jambalaya

serves 4–6

8 oz (250 g) diced ham

1 large yellow onion, roughly chopped

3 cloves garlic, chopped

1 green chile, seeded and chopped

½ green bell pepper (capsicum),
seeded and diced

1 rib (stick) celery, finely chopped

1 can (28 oz/875 g)
chopped tomatoes

2 tablespoons tomato paste

1 teaspoon Worcestershire sauce

½ teaspoon hot chile sauce

1 cup (6½ oz/200 g) uncooked
long-grain white rice

1 lb (500 g) fresh or thawed frozen
uncooked shrimp (prawns)

¼ cup (½ oz/15 g) finely chopped parsley

❖ Place all the ingredients, except the shrimp and parsley, in the slow cooker. Stir well. Put on the lid and cook on Low for 6–8 hours, or until the rice is cooked.

❖ One hour before serving, stir in the shrimp. Replace the lid and cook on Low for 1 hour more, or until the shrimp is cooked. Stir the parsley through the jambalaya and serve hot.

old-fashioned meat loaf

serves 6

2 tablespoons vegetable oil

1 large yellow onion, chopped

1 carrot, peeled and finely chopped

2 cloves garlic, chopped

2 lb (1 kg) lean ground (minced) beef

1½ cups (3 oz/90 g) fresh bread crumbs

2 eggs, lightly beaten

1 teaspoon salt

½ teaspoon ground black pepper

¼ teaspoon dried thyme leaves, crumbled

¼ cup (½ oz/15 g) finely chopped fresh parsley

1 tablespoon Worcestershire sauce

⅔ cup (5 fl oz/160 ml) ketchup (tomato sauce)

½ cup (4 fl oz/125 ml) Basic Tomato Sauce (page 79) or purchased tomato pasta sauce, plus extra to serve (optional)

old-fashioned meat loaf

❖ Warm the vegetable oil in a nonstick frying pan over medium heat. Add the onion and carrot and cook, stirring occasionally, for 4–5 minutes, or until the carrot begins to soften and the onion is almost translucent. Add the garlic and cook for 1 minute longer. Remove from the heat and set aside to cool.

❖ Preheat the oven to 350°F (180°C/Gas Mark 4). Lightly oil a 9- x 5- x 3-inch (23- x 13- x 7.5-cm) loaf pan.

❖ In a large bowl, combine the beef, bread crumbs, and cooled vegetable mixture. In a medium bowl, whisk the eggs with the salt, pepper, thyme, parsley, Worcestershire sauce, and ketchup until combined. Pour the egg mixture over the beef mixture. Using your hands, mix the ingredients together, handling just enough to combine evenly. Do not overmix or the loaf will be too compact and dry.

❖ Pat the meat mixture gently into the prepared loaf pan—don't press too firmly. Pour the tomato sauce evenly over the top and bake for about 1¼ hours, or until the loaf has begun to shrink away from the sides of the pan and a thermometer inserted into the center registers 150°F (66°C). Transfer the meat loaf (in its pan) to a rack and cool for 10 minutes.

❖ Cut the meat loaf into thick slices and, using a spatula, lift out of the pan. Serve warm or cold with more of the tomato sauce, if desired.

basic tomato sauce

makes about 10 cups
(2½ qt/2.5 l)

3 tablespoons olive oil

1 yellow onion, finely chopped

1 carrot, peeled and finely chopped

1 rib (stick) celery, finely chopped

2 large cloves garlic, chopped

2 cans (28 oz/875 g each)
diced tomatoes, drained

1 can (28 oz/875 g)
crushed tomatoes

¼ cup (¼ oz/7 g) chopped parsley

½ bay leaf

1 teaspoon dried oregano,
crumbled

2 teaspoons dried basil, crumbled

1½ cups (12 fl oz/375 ml) water

1 teaspoon salt

¼ teaspoon ground pepper

❖ Heat the olive oil in a large, heavy saucepan over medium heat. Add the onion, carrot, and celery, and cook, stirring occasionally, for 6–8 minutes, or until the vegetables are softened but not browned. Add the garlic and cook for 1 minute longer. Add the diced and crushed tomatoes, parsley, bay leaf, oregano, basil, and water to the pan, partly cover, and reduce the heat to medium–low. Simmer, stirring occasionally, for about 1 hour, or until the flavor is well rounded. Discard the bay leaf.

❖ Purée the mixture in a food processor fitted with a metal blade, or with a hand-held blender, until smooth. Return to the pan, if using a food processor. Stir in the salt and pepper. Continue to simmer briefly over medium–low heat until reduced to the desired consistency. Taste and adjust the seasoning, if necessary. Use immediately, or let cool, cover, and refrigerate for up to 5 days. The sauce can be frozen for up to 2 months.

chile con carne

serves 6

1¼ cups (8 oz/250 g) red
kidney beans

2 tablespoons olive oil

2 medium sweet onions,
finely chopped

2 cloves garlic, chopped

1 red chile, seeded and
finely chopped

2 teaspoons chili powder

1 teaspoon ground cumin

1 lb (500 g) ground
(minced) beef

1 can (28 oz/880 g) chopped
tomatoes

1 tablespoon tomato paste

salt and ground black pepper

✧ Place the beans in a large bowl and cover with water. Leave to soak overnight, then drain. Boil in a saucepan with plenty of water for 15 minutes. Drain.

✧ Heat the oil in a large frying pan. Cook the onion, garlic, and chopped chile for 3 minutes, or until softened. Stir in the chili powder and cumin, and cook for 1 minute more.

✧ Increase the heat and add the beef, stirring and mashing it with a fork until it has changed color.

✧ Stir in the beans, tomatoes, and tomato paste, and season to taste with salt and black pepper. Transfer to the slow cooker. Put on the lid and cook on Low for 8–10 hours, or until the beans are tender. Stir well before serving.

veal shank
with candied shallots

serves 4

1 veal shank (knuckle),
about 2¾ lb (1.4 kg)

3 tablespoons coarse
sea salt

12 large golden
(French) shallots

1 tablespoon peanut oil

1 sprig fresh thyme

3 whole cloves

2½ tablespoons Sauternes
or sweet white muscat wine

salt and ground pepper

Mashed Potatoes (page 66),
to serve

❖ Season the shank well with sea salt and stand for
1 hour. Preheat the oven to 300°F (150°C/Gas Mark 2).
Wash the shank, pat dry, and place in a large cast-iron pot.

❖ Peel and trim the shallots, toss with the oil, and add to
the shank. Add the thyme and cloves. Pour in the wine and
cover the pot.

❖ Cook in the oven, turning the shank 2 or 3 times, for
3 hours, or until the meat is golden, tender, and pulls easily
away from the bone.

❖ Remove the meat and set aside on a dish with the
shallots. Boil the cooking juices until reduced and golden.
Stir in 2 tablespoons water and pour into a sauceboat.

❖ Arrange the shank and candied shallots on a warmed
platter. Serve with Mashed Potatoes, and pass the
sauce separately.

chicken pot pie

serves 8

CHEDDAR PASTRY

2 cups (10 oz/315 g) all-purpose
(plain) flour

3/4 cup (6 oz/185 g) unsalted butter, chilled
and cut into small pieces

1 cup (4 oz/125 g) shredded sharp
Cheddar cheese

1/2 cup (4 fl oz/125 ml) ice water

FILLING

2 1/4 cups (18 fl oz/560 ml) chicken stock

2 skinless, whole chicken breast fillets,
about 1 1/2 lb (750 g) total weight

salt

2 1/2 cups (12 oz/375 g) baby carrots,
cut into 1-inch (2.5-cm) pieces

3 ribs (sticks) celery, thickly sliced

10 oz (315 g) pearl onions, peeled

1 cup (5 oz/155 g) small peas

1/3 cup (3 oz/90 g) unsalted butter

1/2 cup (2 1/2 oz/75 g) all-purpose (plain) flour

1 cup (8 fl oz/250 ml) heavy (double) cream

salt and ground black pepper

1 teaspoon chopped fresh thyme

3 tablespoons chopped fresh chives

3 tablespoons chopped fresh parsley

1 egg, lightly beaten

✤ For the Cheddar pastry, place the flour in a bowl. Using a pastry blender or your fingertips, work in the butter until crumbly. Add the cheese and work in until just blended. Sprinkle the ice water over the pastry dough, a little at a time, and gather the pastry into a ball. Knead lightly until just combined. Wrap in plastic wrap and chill until needed.

✤ For the filling, bring the stock to a simmer in a saucepan over medium heat. Add the chicken and simmer, uncovered, for 15–20 minutes, or until opaque throughout. Remove from the heat and let the chicken cool completely in the liquid. Remove the breasts, reserving the stock. You should have about 2½ cups (20 fl oz/625 ml) stock. Cut the chicken into ¾-inch (2-cm) chunks and set aside.

✤ Bring a saucepan three-fourths full of water to the boil and salt lightly. Add the carrots and cook over medium–high heat for 5–6 minutes. Add the celery, pearl onions, and peas and cook for about 3 minutes longer, or until all are barely tender. Drain well and set aside.

✤ Melt the butter in a saucepan over medium heat. Sprinkle in the flour and whisk for 2–3 minutes, or until the mixture is gently bubbling and smooth; do not brown. Gradually add the reserved stock, whisking constantly, and bring to a simmer. Cook, stirring often, for 4–5 minutes, or until smooth and slightly thickened. Add the cream and cook, stirring occasionally, for about 5 minutes longer, or until the sauce coats the back of the spoon. Remove from the heat, season to taste with salt and pepper, and stir in the thyme, chives, and parsley.

chicken pot pie

❖ Preheat the oven to 400°F (200°C/Gas Mark 5). Add the chicken and vegetables to the sauce and stir to combine. Spoon into a 9- x 13-inch (23- x 33-cm) baking dish and brush the edge of the dish with some of the beaten egg.

❖ On a lightly floured work surface, roll the pastry out into a 10- x 15-inch (25- x 38-cm) rectangle. Lay the pastry over the chicken mixture, pressing the edges firmly onto the dish. Trim away the overhang. Gently knead the dough scraps together, roll out ⅛ inch (3 mm) thick, and cut out several small leaf shapes. Brush the top of the pie with the beaten egg. Using the knife, score the pastry leaves lightly, attach them to the pie pastry, and brush with more egg. Cut 3 slits, each 1 inch (2.5 cm) long, in the pastry near the center of the pie.

❖ Bake for 25–30 minutes, or until golden. Remove from the oven and let stand for 5 minutes, then spoon onto warmed individual plates or into bowls.

beef stew
with winter vegetables

serves 6

½ cup (2½ oz/75 g) all-purpose (plain) flour

3 lb (1.5 kg) beef chuck, cut into
1½-inch (4-cm) cubes

5 tablespoons (3 fl oz/80 ml) olive oil

¼ cup (2 fl oz/60 ml) red wine vinegar

2 large yellow onions, thinly sliced

2 carrots, peeled and thinly sliced

2 cups (16 fl oz/500 ml) beef stock

1 cup (8 fl oz/250 ml) dry red wine

¼ cup (2 fl oz/60 ml) tomato paste

2 cloves garlic, chopped

1 bay leaf

4 sprigs fresh parsley

1 sprig fresh sage or ½ teaspoon dried
sage, crumbled

1 lb (500 g) butternut squash (pumpkin),
peeled, seeded, and cut into
bite-size chunks

10 oz (315 g) pearl onions, peeled fresh
or thawed frozen

½ teaspoon salt

¼ teaspoon ground pepper

1 tablespoon finely chopped fresh parsley

beef stew with winter vegetables

Butternut squash is added to this thick, meaty stew for sweetness and its natural ability to thicken the stew.

Refrigerating the stew overnight will further develop the flavor, while also making it easier to remove any excess fat.

◈ Spread the flour on a large plate. Coat the beef with the flour and shake off the excess.

◈ Heat 4 tablespoons of the olive oil in a large, heavy, nonstick pot over medium–high heat. Working in batches if necessary, cook the beef for 5–7 minutes, or until it is browned evenly on all sides. Using tongs or a slotted spoon, transfer the beef to a plate.

◈ Add the vinegar to the pot and deglaze over medium–high heat, stirring to dislodge any browned bits from the bottom of the pot. Add the remaining 1 tablespoon oil and the yellow onions and cook over medium–high heat, stirring occasionally, for about 15 minutes, or until nicely browned.

◈ Add the carrots to the pot and cook for about 3 minutes, or until slightly softened. Add the beef stock, wine, tomato paste, garlic, bay leaf, parsley, and sage.

beef stew with winter vegetables

◈ Reduce the heat to medium–low, cover, and simmer, stirring occasionally, for 1½–1¾ hours, or until the meat is almost tender.

◈ Add the butternut squash, cover, and continue to simmer for about 15 minutes, or until both the squash and the meat are tender when pierced with a fork. Add the pearl onions and cook for about 5 minutes longer, or until just tender. Stir in the salt, pepper, and parsley.

◈ Spoon onto warmed individual plates or into bowls and serve immediately.

recipe **hint**

For a change of flavor, substitute potatoes, parsnip, or okra, or a mixture of any of these vegetables, for the butternut squash. The thickening abilities of all these vegetables are similar. If the stew is still not thick enough for your liking, mix a little all-purpose (plain) flour to a paste with a little water and stir it into the stew. Cook for 2–3 minutes, or until there is no taste of raw flour.

all-in-together
beef and vegetables

serves 6

1/4 cup (1 1/2 oz/45 g) all-purpose (plain) flour

1/4 cup (2 fl oz/60 ml) soy sauce

2 teaspoons Worcestershire sauce

1 teaspoon dried thyme leaves, crumbled

2 lb (1 kg) stewing beef (blade or chuck), cut into 1-inch (2.5-cm) cubes

1 yellow onion, sliced

2 carrots, cut into 1-inch (2.5-cm) pieces

2 ribs (sticks) celery, cut into 1-inch (2.5-cm) pieces

4 oz (125 g) mushrooms, thickly sliced

1/2 cup (4 fl oz/125 ml) red wine

1/2 cup (4 fl oz/125 ml) beef stock

salt and ground black pepper

1/2 cup (1/2 oz/15 g) chopped fresh parsley

❖ Combine the flour, soy sauce, Worcestershire sauce, and thyme leaves and mix until smooth. Pour into the slow cooker. Toss the beef cubes in the mixture, stirring until well coated.

❖ Stir in the onion, carrots, celery, mushrooms, wine, and stock. Season to taste with salt and pepper.

❖ Put on the lid and cook on Low for 8–10 hours, or High for 4–5 hours. Sprinkle with parsley and serve with Mashed Potatoes (page 66) or steamed rice.

turkey wrapped in tortillas

1 can (16 oz/500 g) dark plums,
drained and pitted

½ cup (4 fl oz/125 ml) fresh orange juice

½ cup (1½ oz/45 g) chopped green
(spring) onions, plus 2 extra, thinly sliced

1 tablespoon chopped fresh ginger

¼ teaspoon ground mixed spice

1 lb (500 g) turkey breast meat,
sliced into strips 2 inches (5 cm) long

1½ cups (4½ oz/140 g) finely shredded
cabbage

1 carrot, peeled and grated

6 flour tortillas, 7 inches (18 cm) across

1 avocado, thinly sliced

❖ Mash or process the plums until almost smooth. Pour into the slow cooker and stir in the orange juice, chopped green onion, ginger, and mixed spice.

❖ Place the turkey strips on top of the mixture. Put on the lid and cook on Low for 3–4 hours.

❖ Meanwhile, combine the cabbage, carrot, and sliced green onion in a large bowl.

❖ Evenly divide the turkey strips over the tortillas. Spoon over a little of the plum sauce and top with the combined cabbage mixture and the sliced avocado. Roll up the tortillas, completely enclosing the filling. Serve the remaining plum sauce separately as a dip.

beer and beef brisket

serves 6–8

12 oz (375 ml) flat beer

1 tablespoon pickling spices

1 teaspoon dry mustard

2 sprigs fresh thyme

4 lb (2 kg) beef brisket

2 carrots, cut into 1½-inch
(4-cm) pieces

1 parsnip, cut into 1½-inch
(4-cm) pieces

1 large sweet potato,
peeled and cut into
1½-inch (4-cm) pieces

salt and ground black pepper

❧ In a large nonmetallic bowl, combine the beer, spices, mustard, and thyme sprigs. Trim any fat from the meat and pat dry with paper towels. Place the beef in the mixture and add enough water just to cover. Refrigerate for several hours or overnight.

❧ Put the beef in the slow cooker and pour over half the marinade, including the thyme sprigs. Surround the meat with the vegetables. Season with salt and pepper.

❧ Put on the lid and cook on Low for 12–14 hours, or High for 7–10 hours. Serve hot, sliced, on a platter with the vegetables and some of the juices.

oven-braised chicken
with vegetables

serves 4

1 chicken, 3½–4 lb (1.75–2 kg)

1 yellow onion, cut in half

2 leeks, including tops,
trimmed and washed

1 head iceberg lettuce, cored and
sliced lengthwise

2 carrots, peeled and chopped

2 green bell peppers (capsicums),
seeds and ribs removed,
coarsely chopped

2 tablespoons (1 oz/30 g)
unsalted butter, at room
temperature

salt and ground pepper

½ cup (4 fl oz/125 ml) each
dry white wine and chicken stock

❖ Preheat the oven to 375°F (190°C/Gas Mark 4). Trim
any excess fat from the chicken. Pat dry with paper
towels and place the onion halves inside. Set aside.

❖ Cut the leeks in half lengthwise and thickly slice
crosswise. Place the lettuce, carrots, leeks, and bell
peppers in the bottom of a heavy, ovenproof pot.

❖ Rub the outside of the chicken with the butter and
salt and pepper to taste. Place it in the pot, breast side
up. Add the wine and stock. Cover and bake in the
oven for 1 hour. Uncover and continue to cook for
30 minutes longer, or until the chicken is tender.

❖ Transfer the chicken to a warmed deep platter.
Arrange the vegetables around the bird and spoon
the pan juices over both. Carve at the table.

barbecue-style braised
short ribs

serves 6

Beef short ribs are a highly flavorsome cut, and slow cooking makes the meat so tender it almost falls off the bone. Parboiling the meat before cooking reduces the amount of fat while retaining the flavor. Serve with a generous helping of Candied Yams (page 240).

5 lb (2.5 kg) lean beef short ribs, cut into pieces about 4 inches (10 cm) long

1 teaspoon salt, plus extra to taste

½ teaspoon ground pepper, plus extra to taste

2 tablespoons vegetable oil

2 yellow onions, thickly sliced into rings

2 carrots, peeled and sliced

4 cloves garlic, coarsely chopped

2 cups (16 fl oz/500 ml) Tomato Sauce (page 247)

1 cup (8 fl oz/250 ml) purchased barbecue sauce

1 cup (8 fl oz/250 ml) beef stock

❖ Bring a large pot three-fourths full of water to the boil. Plunge the short ribs into the water, partly cover, and simmer for 20 minutes. Drain, then pat dry with paper towels. Season the ribs with the 1 teaspoon salt and ½ teaspoon pepper.

❖ Preheat the oven to 325°F (160°C/Gas Mark 3).

❖ Heat the vegetable oil in a large nonstick frying pan over medium–high heat. Using tongs to turn them, cook the ribs for about 5 minutes, or until browned evenly on all sides. Transfer the ribs to paper towels to drain briefly, then place them in a large, heavy pot or baking dish.

❖ Cook the onions in the same frying pan over medium–high heat, stirring frequently, for about 5 minutes, or until browned. Add the carrots and cook for 2–3 minutes longer, or until slightly softened. Add the garlic and cook for 1 minute. Stir in the tomato sauce, barbecue sauce, and beef stock. Reduce the heat to low and simmer for 1 minute to blend the flavors. Pour the tomato sauce mixture over the short ribs and turn to coat evenly.

❖ Bake the ribs, turning every 45 minutes, for about 2½ hours, or until the meat is very tender. Season to taste with salt and pepper. Serve immediately on warmed individual plates.

roast chicken with provençal vegetables

serves 4

2 tablespoons (1 oz/30 g) unsalted butter,
at room temperature

1 teaspoon chopped fresh thyme,
plus 5 or 6 sprigs

salt and ground black pepper

1 roasting chicken, about 3½ lb (1.75 kg)

1 head garlic

olive oil

1 cup (5 oz/155 g) peeled and cubed
eggplant (aubergine)

1 small fennel bulb, trimmed and cut into
fourths lengthwise

8 bottled marinated artichoke hearts,
drained and halved lengthwise

1 small zucchini (courgette),
halved lengthwise

4 boiling onions, root ends trimmed

2 small plum (Roma) tomatoes,
halved lengthwise

8 black olives, cured in oil and herbs

1 cup (8 fl oz/250 ml) water

❖ Preheat the oven to 400°F (200°C/Gas Mark 5).

❖ Combine the butter in a small bowl with the chopped thyme, ¼ teaspoon salt, and ¼ teaspoon pepper. Using a rubber spatula, blend together well. Season the inside of the chicken with ¼ teaspoon salt. Spread the butter mixture over the outside of the chicken, truss it securely, and place in a large roasting pan.

❖ Sprinkle the garlic with ¼ teaspoon salt and 1 teaspoon olive oil. Wrap in aluminum foil and place in the roasting pan with the chicken. Toss the eggplant in a bowl with ½ teaspoon salt. Let stand for 10 minutes, then drizzle with about 2 tablespoons olive oil. Toss well to coat.

❖ Bring a saucepan of water to the boil, add the fennel, and boil for 4 minutes. Drain and place in a large bowl with the artichokes, zucchini, onions, tomatoes, ¼ teaspoon each salt and pepper, 2 tablespoons olive oil, thyme sprigs, and the eggplant. Toss to coat evenly.

❖ Roast the chicken for 10 minutes. Remove from the oven and reduce the temperature to 375°F (190°C/Gas Mark 4). Arrange the vegetables around the chicken and roast for 30 minutes. Stir the vegetables, add the olives to the pan, and baste the chicken with some of the pan juices. Roast for about 10 minutes more, or until the vegetables are browned and tender and the juices run clear when the thickest part of the chicken thigh is pierced with a knife. Transfer the chicken to a warmed platter and arrange the vegetables and garlic around it.

❖ Skim off any excess fat from the roasting pan, add the water, and deglaze the pan over medium heat, stirring to dislodge any browned bits from the bottom. Pour into a small saucepan and cook over high heat for about 5 minutes, or until reduced slightly. Strain through a fine-mesh sieve into a pitcher and pour over the vegetables. Carve the chicken at the table.

braised
beef short ribs
with mushrooms

serves 4–6

2 white onions

1 leek, trimmed and well rinsed

1 rib (stick) celery

5 sprigs fresh parsley

5 sprigs fresh thyme

2 bay leaves

2 tablespoons olive oil

4 lb (2 kg) beef short ribs

1 cup (5 oz/155 g) peeled and diced carrot

2 ribs (sticks) celery, diced

1 tablespoon chopped garlic

1½ cups (12 fl oz/375 ml) dry red wine

1 cup (6 oz/185 g) peeled, seeded, and diced tomato

5 cups (40 fl oz/1.25 liters) beef stock

2 teaspoons salt

1 teaspoon whole peppercorns

¼ cup (2 oz/60 g) unsalted butter

1 lb (500 g) fresh mushrooms, such as morel, chanterelle, or porcini, brushed clean and sliced

1 teaspoon chopped fresh parsley

1 teaspoon chopped fresh thyme

✧ Cut each onion through the stem end into fourths, leaving each fourth attached at the root end. To make a bouquet garni, tie the leek, celery rib, parsley, thyme, and bay leaves together securely with kitchen string.

✧ Heat the olive oil in a large, heavy saucepan over high heat. Place enough of the short ribs in the pan to cover the bottom. Cook, turning once, for 2–3 minutes on each side, or until well browned all over. Transfer to a platter. Repeat with the remaining ribs.

✧ Add the carrot, celery, and garlic and cook for about 5 minutes, or until lightly colored. Drain off any excess fat and deglaze the pan with the red wine, stirring to dislodge any browned bits from the bottom of the pan. Add the tomato and the onions to the pan. Pour in the beef stock, add the prepared bouquet garni, the salt, and peppercorns, and return to the boil. Return the short ribs to the pan, reduce the heat to low, cover, and cook for 2–2½ hours, or until the meat pulls easily away from the bones.

✧ While the ribs are cooking, heat a large frying pan over medium heat. Add the butter and cook the mushrooms for 4–5 minutes, or until very tender. Remove from the heat and set aside.

✧ When the meat is ready, use tongs to transfer the ribs to a warmed deep platter. Transfer the onions to the platter as well, arranging them around the meat; keep warm. Strain the cooking liquid through a fine-mesh sieve into a clean saucepan and heat on medium–high. Skim off any oil from the surface and allow to boil until the liquid is reduced by one-third. Add the mushrooms and any accumulated juices, the parsley, and thyme, and bring to the boil. Boil for 5 minutes, then pour over the ribs and serve hot.

roast
rack of pork
with apples and onions

serves 6

1 rack of pork with 12 chops, trimmed,
leaving a layer of fat about ½ inch
(1 cm) thick, and with bones frenched
(see Glossary, page 311)

2 cloves garlic, sliced paper-thin

1 teaspoon chopped fresh thyme

1 teaspoon salt

½ teaspoon cracked pepper

½ cup (4 oz/125 g) unsalted butter

2 white onions, halved and sliced

1½ cups (12 fl oz/375 ml) unfiltered
apple cider

2 tablespoons cider vinegar

1 tablespoon honey

1 cinnamon stick, about 3 inches (7.5 cm)

1 bay leaf

3 sprigs fresh thyme

2 red apples, cored and cut into
small wedges

1 tablespoon sugar

2 cups (16 fl oz/500 ml) water

❧ Preheat the oven to 400°F (200°C/Gas Mark 5). Make a series of small incisions in the fat and flesh of the pork, and insert a slice of garlic into each slit. Sprinkle the chopped thyme, salt, and pepper all over the pork, then rub the seasonings into the meat. Roast in a roasting pan for 20 minutes. Reduce the temperature to 350°F (180°C/Gas Mark 4) and roast for 40–50 minutes, or until an instant-read thermometer inserted into the center of the meat, away from the bone, registers 150°F (66°C), or until a chop is pale pink when cut to the center.

❧ While the pork is roasting, melt half the butter in a large frying pan over medium heat and cook the onion slices for about 3 minutes, or until slightly wilted. Add the apple cider, cider vinegar, honey, cinnamon stick, bay leaf, and thyme sprigs. Bring to the boil, reduce the heat to low, and simmer for about 20 minutes, or until the liquid has evaporated and the onions are golden brown.

❧ Meanwhile, melt the remaining butter in a medium frying pan over low heat. Add the apple wedges and increase the heat to medium. Add the sugar and cook for about 5 minutes, or until the apples are caramelized. Remove from the heat. When the onions are ready, combine with the apples, discarding the bay leaf and thyme sprigs. Cover and keep warm.

❧ When the pork is ready, transfer to a serving platter. Skim the fat from the pan juices and heat the pan on the stove top on medium–high. Add the water and deglaze the pan by stirring to dislodge any browned bits from the bottom of the pan. Pour the juices into a small saucepan and boil over high heat until slightly reduced. Pour through a fine-mesh sieve into a small bowl.

❧ To serve, spoon the apple-onion mixture around the edges of the serving platter and pour the reduced pan juices over the pork. Carve at the table.

italian sausage
casserole

serves 4–6

1 lb (500 g) hot or mild Italian sausages

1 sweet onion, cut into thin wedges

½ red bell pepper (capsicum),
seeded and thickly sliced

½ teaspoon fennel seeds

1 small fennel bulb, trimmed and
cut into thin wedges

1 medium zucchini (courgette), sliced

2 oz (60 g) fresh mushrooms, sliced

1 can (14 oz/440 g) Italian-style
whole tomatoes, undrained

1 tablespoon tomato paste

1 teaspoon sugar

salt and ground black pepper

shredded basil leaves, to serve

❖ Cut sausage into 1½-inch (4-cm) pieces. Heat a large frying pan, add the sausage, and cook, stirring, for 3–4 minutes, or until lightly browned. Remove and set aside.

❖ Add the onion wedges, bell pepper, and fennel seeds to the pan juices in the frying pan. Cook for 2–3 minutes to soften a little. Put in the slow cooker along with the sausage, fennel wedges, zucchini, and mushrooms. Stir through the tomatoes and their juice, tomato paste, and sugar, and season to taste with salt and pepper.

❖ Put on the lid and cook on Low for 5–6 hours. Sprinkle with shredded basil leaves. Serve hot with sliced Italian bread.

steak and onions with sour cream

serves 4–6

2 lb (1 kg) round steak, cut into
4-inch (10-cm) pieces

¼ cup (1½ oz/45 g) all-purpose
(plain) flour

2 tablespoons vegetable oil

2 tablespoons (1 oz/30 g) butter

2 large yellow onions,
cut into thin rings

3 cloves garlic, chopped

1 cup (8 fl oz/250 ml) beef stock

2 teaspoons Worcestershire sauce

1 teaspoon soy sauce

salt and ground black pepper

¾ cup (6 fl oz/185 ml) sour cream

½ cup (½ oz/15 g)
chopped fresh parsley

❖ Pat the steak pieces dry with paper towels. Put the flour in a plastic bag, add the meat, and shake to coat evenly with the flour.

❖ Heat half the oil and half the butter in a large pan. Fry half the meat, stirring, for 3–4 minutes, or until the pieces are golden brown. Place in the slow cooker. Repeat with remaining oil, butter, and meat.

❖ Add the onion rings and garlic to the frying pan, adding a little more oil, if necessary. Cook, stirring, for 2–3 minutes. Add the stock, Worcestershire sauce, and soy sauce. Stir to deglaze the pan, then add to the meat in the slow cooker.

❖ Season with salt and pepper. Put on the lid and cook on Low for 7–9 hours. Stir in the sour cream and parsley and serve hot with boiled potatoes.

pot-au-feu

serves 10

Here is a classic French slow-cooked, boiled dinner, prepared in a quantity large enough for a big family-style meal. It also makes an excellent choice for casual entertaining, since it conjures both a first and second course from the one pot.

1 beef chuck roast or beef brisket, 3½ lb (1.75 kg)

1 lb (500 g) beef marrow bones

1 yellow onion, studded with 2 whole cloves

1 roasting chicken, about 4 lb (2 kg), trussed

4 ribs (sticks) celery

3 leeks, trimmed, split lengthwise and well rinsed

3 carrots, peeled and cut into 3-inch (7.5-cm) lengths

2 parsnips, peeled and cut into 3-inch (7.5-cm) lengths

1 turnip, peeled and cut into fourths

1 tablespoon salt, plus extra to serve

1 teaspoon dried thyme

2 bay leaves

6 sprigs fresh parsley

8 whole peppercorns

10 slices French bread

Cornichons (French-style pickles)

Dijon mustard

❖ Place the beef and the beef bones in a 10 qt (10 l) stockpot, add water to cover, and bring slowly to the boil over medium–high heat. Boil for 5 minutes, skimming any scum off the surface. Reduce the heat to medium–low, add the onion, and simmer, uncovered, for 3 hours.

❖ Add the chicken to the pot, adding water, if needed, to cover the chicken. Return the liquid to the boil, boil for 5 minutes, and skim any scum off the surface. Reduce the heat to low and add the celery, leeks, carrots, parsnips, turnip, salt, thyme, bay leaves, parsley, and peppercorns. Simmer, uncovered, for about 1½ hours, or until the chicken juices run clear when it is pierced with a knife and a knife blade can be inserted into the beef without resistance.

❖ About 20 minutes before the meats are ready, preheat the oven to 300°F (150°C/Gas Mark 2). Place the bread slices on a baking sheet and bake for about 10 minutes, or until crisped. Remove from the oven and set aside. Reduce the oven temperature as low as possible.

❖ Using tongs, transfer the chicken and the beef to a large ovenproof platter. Using a slotted spoon, transfer the vegetables to the same platter. Cover and place in the oven. Line a large sieve with cheesecloth (muslin) and strain the pan juices through it into a bowl. Discard the beef bones or reserve for another use. Wipe out the stockpot and add the strained juices to it. Bring just to a boil and remove from the heat.

❖ To serve, place the crisped bread slices in shallow soup bowls, ladle hot stock over the top, and serve as a first course. For the second course, carve the beef thinly, and cut the chicken into small pieces. Serve with the vegetables, spooning a small amount of the stock over each portion. Accompany with cornichons, mustard, and salt on the side.

stuffed breast of veal

serves 6–8

VEAL BREAST

1 veal breast, 5–6 lb (2.5–3 kg)—ask your butcher to bone it, reserving the bones, and cut a pocket in it

¼ cup (2 fl oz/60 ml) olive oil

2½ cups (20 fl oz/625 ml) chicken stock

½ cup (4 fl oz/125 ml) dry white wine

1 small white onion, coarsely chopped

1 small carrot, peeled and sliced

1 bay leaf

1 tablespoon chopped garlic

1½ cups (9 oz/280 g) finely chopped tomatoes

2 teaspoons chopped fresh parsley

STUFFING

¼ cup (2 fl oz/60 ml) olive oil

1 large white onion, finely diced

6 cups (15 oz/470 g) fresh white bread crumbs

2 tablespoons chopped fresh parsley

1 tablespoon fresh thyme leaves

¾ lb (375 g) ground (minced) pork, turkey, or veal

¾ cup (6 fl oz/180 ml) heavy (double) cream

2 eggs

1½ teaspoons salt

½ teaspoon ground pepper

¼ teaspoon ground nutmeg

⅛ teaspoon ground cloves

❖ For the stuffing, heat the oil in a large frying pan over high heat. Add the onion and cook for about 2 minutes, or until tender and slightly translucent. Reduce the heat to medium and add the bread crumbs, parsley, and thyme. Stir until the bread crumbs are well coated. Transfer to a large bowl and let cool. Add the ground meat, cream, eggs, salt, pepper, nutmeg, and cloves, and mix by hand until evenly combined.

❖ Preheat the oven to 325°F (160°C/Gas Mark 3).

❖ For the veal breast, pack the stuffing into the pocket. Close the opening securely.

❖ Heat a large, heavy frying pan over high heat for 3 minutes, add the oil, and brown the stuffed veal breast for 3–4 minutes on each side. Transfer to a platter.

❖ Add the chicken stock and wine to the pan, bring to a boil, and deglaze by stirring to dislodge any browned bits from the bottom of the pan.

❖ Pour the contents of the frying pan into a roasting pan with a cover—it should be large enough to accommodate the veal breast. Add the onion, carrot, bay leaf, reserved veal bones, garlic, and tomatoes. Place the veal breast on top of the vegetables, cover, and cook in the oven for 2 hours.

❖ Uncover and baste the breast with the pan juices. Continue to cook, uncovered, for about 30 minutes longer, or until tender—a thin-bladed knife inserted into the breast should meet with little resistance and the basting juices will form an attractive glaze.

stuffed breast of veal

Arguably the most flavorsome cut of the calf, veal breast is delicious served with green haricot beans. When your butcher bones the breast for you, ask for the bones to add to the baking pan. They bring added richness to the flavor.

❖ Transfer to a large platter. Strain the contents of the pan through a fine-mesh sieve placed over a bowl. Add the parsley and keep warm.

❖ Slice the veal breast and place 2 slices on each warmed individual plate. Spoon some of the braising sauce over the slices and serve immediately.

beef and bean
sloppy joes

serves 4

2 tablespoons vegetable oil

2 sweet onions, thinly sliced

1 green bell pepper (capsicum),
seeded and chopped

3 cloves garlic, chopped

2 teaspoons chili powder

1 lb (500 g) lean ground (minced) beef

1 can (14 oz/440 g) red kidney beans,
rinsed and drained

1 cup (8 oz/250 g) tomato pasta sauce

2 tablespoons Worcestershire sauce

2 tablespoons ketchup (tomato sauce)

2 tablespoons mustard

4 hamburger buns, split and toasted

❖ Heat the oil on medium heat in a large frying pan and cook the onions, chopped bell pepper, and garlic for 2–3 minutes, or until softened. Increase the heat to high and stir in the chili powder and ground beef. Cook, stirring, for 3–4 minutes, or until the meat is lightly browned. Break up any lumps with a fork.

❖ Remove from the heat and stir in the beans, tomato sauce, Worcestershire sauce, ketchup, and mustard.

❖ Transfer to the slow cooker. Put on the lid and cook on Low for 6–8 hours. Spoon onto the hamburger buns and serve.

pork sausage
with rice and broccoli

serves 4–6

1 tablespoon vegetable oil

1 red (Spanish) onion, chopped

1 rib (stick) celery, chopped

4 thick slices (rashers) rindless
bacon, cut into ¾-inch (2-cm) cubes

1 lb (500 g) thin pork sausages,
pricked several times with a fork

1 cup (6½ oz/200 g) uncooked
long-grain white rice

2½ cups (20 fl oz/625 ml) chicken
or beef stock

2 cups (4 oz/125 g) broccoli florets

salt and ground black pepper

❖ Heat the oil in a large frying pan and cook the red onion and celery for 2–3 minutes. Transfer to the slow cooker with a slotted spoon.

❖ Add the bacon cubes and sausages to the frying pan. Cook, stirring, for 2–3 minutes, or until lightly browned. Use scissors to cut sausages into 2-inch (5-cm) pieces. Add to the slow cooker.

❖ Stir the rice, stock, and broccoli florets into the slow cooker. Season to taste with salt and pepper. Put on the lid and cook on Low for 5–6 hours, or until the rice is cooked. Serve hot.

roast chicken
with bread and garlic

serves 4

1 roasting chicken, about 4 lb (2 kg)

salt and ground black pepper

*6 whole cloves garlic, plus
2 cloves, sliced paper-thin*

*1 day-old baguette, sliced into strips
about 5 inches (13 cm) long and
1 inch (2.5 cm) thick*

*2 tablespoons (1 oz/30 g) unsalted
butter, at room temperature*

2 sprigs fresh thyme

1 lemon, cut in half

1 tablespoon olive oil

1 cup (8 fl oz/250 ml) water

*¼ cup (2 fl oz/60 ml) veal
or chicken stock*

❖ Preheat the oven to 450°F (220°C/Gas Mark 6).

❖ Rinse the chicken thoroughly with water and pat dry with paper towels. Rub inside and out with salt and pepper.

❖ Cut one of the whole garlic cloves in half and rub the cut sides of the clove over each baguette strip. Spread the strips on all sides with some of the butter.

❖ Using the tip of a sharp knife, make at least 12 small incisions in the skin of the chicken on all sides. Slip 1 thin garlic slice into each incision, between the skin and the meat.

❖ Rub the inside of the chicken with the remaining butter, and press the remaining thin garlic slices against the cavity walls. Stuff the

roast chicken with bread and garlic

bread strips into the chicken cavity and, using kitchen string, truss the chicken by tying the legs together and then tying the legs and wings tightly against the body. Tuck the 2 thyme sprigs between the chicken thighs and the body.

❖ Place the chicken in a roasting pan, breast side down, with the lemon halves alongside. Drizzle the olive oil over the chicken and turn breast side up. Scatter the remaining 5 whole garlic cloves around the chicken.

❖ Roast the chicken for 15 minutes. Turn breast side down and roast for 10 minutes longer. Add the water to the roasting pan and continue to roast for 10–20 minutes longer, or until the juices run clear when the thigh is pierced with a knife in the thickest part.

❖ Transfer the chicken to a cutting board. Snip the strings and remove them. Remove the bread from the cavity; arrange it around the edge of a serving platter or place it in a separate dish. Carve the chicken into 8 serving pieces and arrange them in the center of the platter, or place the whole chicken on the platter and carve it at the table.

❖ Remove the lemon halves from the roasting pan. Place the pan over high heat, squeeze the lemons into the pan, and deglaze it by stirring to dislodge any browned bits from the bottom of the pan. Add the stock and bring to the boil. Pour the sauce through a fine-mesh sieve into a small serving pitcher.

❖ Place the pitcher of sauce alongside the chicken and serve at once.

stuffed, boned chicken

serves 6–8

1 large chicken, about 4 lb (2 kg)

2 boneless, skinless chicken breast halves, each about 4 oz (125 g)

1 thick slice cooked ham

1 small onion, very finely chopped

2 tablespoons finely chopped parsley

1 tablespoon finely chopped red bell pepper (capsicum)

2 tablespoons chopped stuffed olives

¾ teaspoon salt

½ teaspoon ground black pepper

½ teaspoon dried mixed herbs

1 large egg

2 tablespoons (1 oz/30 g) butter or 2 slices (rashers) bacon

stuffed, boned chicken

❖ Preheat the oven to 350°F (180°C/Gas Mark 4).

❖ Using a small knife, bone the chicken, leaving the skin in one piece. Start at the neck and work the knife between the bones and the meat. Sever the wing and drumstick joints at the carcass. Pull or cut the chicken meat off the bones and cut into small chunks. Freeze the bones and carcass for later use in stock or soup.

❖ Cut the chicken breasts and ham into small chunks. Process the ham and all the chicken meat in a food processor until smooth. Add the onion, parsley, bell pepper, olives, salt, pepper, herbs, and egg. Process until well mixed but retaining some texture.

❖ Stuff the chicken with the mixture and sew up the openings or close with skewers. Rub the skin of the chicken with salt and pepper, and squeeze gently to reshape. Place in a buttered oven dish just large enough to accommodate the chicken comfortably. Spread the butter over the top, or cover with the strips of bacon. Bake the chicken in the oven for about 1 hour. To test for doneness, pierce with a fine skewer—the chicken is done if the juices run clear with no tinge of pink.

❖ Increase the oven heat, remove the bacon strips, and cook for a few minutes more to brown the top. Remove from the oven. The chicken may be served hot or cold. If serving hot, allow to rest in a warm place for 5–6 minutes before slicing to serve.

❖ The chicken can be fully prepared and refrigerated or frozen until needed. If frozen, thaw slowly before cooking.

hungarian veal stew

serves 4

2 tablespoons olive oil

1 large yellow onion, thinly sliced

2 cloves garlic, finely chopped

2 lb (1 kg) boneless
veal shoulder, cut into
1-inch (2.5-cm) cubes

2 tablespoons all-purpose
(plain) flour

1 tablespoon sweet paprika

½ teaspoon dried
thyme leaves

1 can (14 oz/440 g)
crushed tomatoes

1 tablespoon tomato paste

salt and ground black pepper

1 cup (8 fl oz/250 ml) sour cream

chives, to garnish (optional)

❖ Heat half the oil in a large frying pan and cook the onion and garlic for 2–3 minutes, or until softened. Transfer to the slow cooker with a slotted spoon.

❖ Pat the veal cubes dry with paper towels. Use the remaining oil to fry the veal over high heat in 2 or 3 batches. Transfer to the slow cooker.

❖ Combine the flour, paprika, and thyme. Sprinkle over the veal and onions and mix to coat thoroughly. Stir in the tomatoes and tomato paste and season to taste with salt and pepper. Put on the lid and cook on Low for 8–10 hours, or High for 5–6 hours. Stir in the sour cream 30 minutes before serving. Serve on buttered pasta, garnished with chives.

roast garlic chicken

serves 4–6

1 chicken, about 3 lb (1.5 kg)

2 tablespoons fresh
sage leaves

2 whole heads garlic, cloves
separated and peeled

3 tablespoons (1½ oz/50 g)
butter, at room temperature

salt and ground black pepper

1 tablespoon olive oil

½ cup (4 fl oz/125 ml)
white wine

½ cup (4 fl oz/125 ml)
chicken stock

extra sage leaves, to garnish

❖ Pat the chicken dry inside and out with paper towels. Place the sage leaves and 6 cloves of garlic in the cavity. Rub half the butter all over the chicken and season well with salt and pepper.

❖ Heat the remaining butter and the oil in a large frying pan. Brown the chicken on all sides until evenly colored. Transfer to the slow cooker. Pour off and discard most of the fat from the frying pan. Add the white wine and stock and deglaze the pan by stirring to remove any browned bits from the bottom of the pan.

❖ Pour the liquid from the pan over the chicken and surround with the remaining garlic cloves. Put on the lid and cook on High for 5–6 hours.

❖ Cut the chicken in portions and serve with the whole garlic cloves. Garnish with extra sage leaves.

shrimp risotto

serves 4

1 tablespoon vegetable oil

1 large sweet onion, finely chopped

1 rib (stick) celery, finely chopped

3 oz (90 g) button mushrooms, finely chopped

2 tomatoes, skinned, seeded, and chopped

1¼ cups (8 oz/250 g) uncooked long-grain white rice

3½ cups (28 fl oz/875 ml) chicken stock

8 oz (250 g) fresh or frozen shrimp (prawns)

½ cup (½ oz/15 g) chopped parsley, plus some whole leaves, to garnish (optional)

❖ Heat the oil in a large frying pan and cook the onion and celery for 2–3 minutes. Transfer to the slow cooker with a slotted spoon.

❖ Place all the remaining ingredients, except the shrimp and parsley, in the slow cooker. Stir well. Put on the lid and cook on Low for 5–6 hours, or until the rice is cooked.

❖ One hour before serving, stir through the uncooked shrimp. Replace the lid and continue cooking until the rice is cooked. Stir through the parsley and serve the risotto hot, garnished with whole parsley leaves, if desired.

drunken pork
with cabbage and pears

serves 4–6

bouquet garni (see Glossary, page 310)

2 white onions, diced

2 carrots, peeled and diced

2 ribs (sticks) celery, diced

3 cloves garlic

30 whole black peppercorns

5 cups (40 fl oz/1.25 l) dry red wine,
such as Cabernet or Merlot

salt to taste, plus 1 tablespoon extra

3 lb (1.5 kg) boneless pork shoulder,
cut into 1-inch (2.5-cm) cubes

6 tablespoons (3 fl oz/100 ml) olive oil

4 cups (32 fl oz/1 liter) veal
or chicken stock

1 head green cabbage, thinly sliced

3 tablespoons unsalted butter

¼ vanilla bean, split in half lengthwise

3 ripe but firm pears, such as Comice,
cored, peeled, and cut into ¾-inch
(2-cm) cubes

½ cup (½ oz/15 g) chopped fresh parsley

drunken pork with cabbage and pears

❖ In a large, shallow, nonreactive dish, combine the bouquet garni, onions, carrots, celery, garlic, peppercorns, all but ½ cup (4 fl oz/125 ml) of the red wine, and salt to taste. Stir to mix. Add the pork and turn to coat evenly. Cover and refrigerate in the marinade overnight, or for at least 5 hours.

❖ Drain the meat and vegetables in a sieve, reserving the marinade in a small saucepan. Bring the marinade to the boil, then remove from the heat and set aside. Separate the meat from the vegetables.

❖ Warm 2 tablespoons of olive oil in a frying pan on high heat. Pat the meat dry with paper towels. Working in small batches and adding more oil as needed, cook the meat for about 2 minutes, browning on all sides. Transfer the meat to a large saucepan.

❖ Add the reserved vegetables to the same frying pan and cook over medium–high heat for about 5 minutes, or until they begin to brown. Transfer the vegetables to the saucepan with the meat, along with the reserved marinade.

❖ Bring to a boil over high heat and boil for about 10 minutes, or until reduced by half. Add the veal stock and return to the boil. Reduce heat to medium and simmer, uncovered, for 50–60 minutes, or until the pork is tender.

❖ Meanwhile, fill another large saucepan two-thirds full with water, add the 1 tablespoon salt, and bring to the boil. Add the cabbage, return to the boil, and cook for about 2 minutes, or until wilted.

drunken pork with cabbage and pears

❖ Drain the cabbage, rinse with cold water to refresh, and drain again.

❖ Melt the butter in a clean frying pan over medium heat. Add the cabbage and cook for 2 minutes. Remove from the heat and set aside.

❖ In another small frying pan, combine the reserved ½ cup (4 fl oz/125 ml) red wine, the vanilla bean, and the pears and bring to the boil. Reduce the heat to medium and simmer, turning the fruit every few minutes, for 5–10 minutes, or until tender.

❖ Drain the meat and vegetables in a sieve, reserving the juices in a bowl. Cover the juices to keep them warm. Separate the pork from the vegetables; discard the vegetables.

❖ Arrange a bed of cabbage on a warmed platter. Place the pork on top of the cabbage, and pour the reserved juices over the top. Scatter the poached pear cubes around the meat. Garnish with parsley and serve at once.

recipe variations

Red cabbage can be substituted in this recipe and prepared in the same way as green cabbage or, for a Hungarian touch, use canned sauerkraut. The sharpness of the sauerkraut is a good foil for the richness of the pork. Warm the sauerkraut, drain well, and arrange on a warmed platter. Place the pork on top and serve.

braised
veal short ribs
with parsnips

serves 4

SHORT RIBS

3 tablespoons olive oil

3 lb (1.5 kg) veal short ribs

2 carrots, peeled and diced

1 large white onion, diced

1 rib (stick) celery

6 cloves garlic

1 cup (8 fl oz/250 ml) dry white wine

5 cups (40 fl oz/1.25 l) veal or beef stock

bouquet garni (see Glossary, page 310)

1 teaspoon salt

1 teaspoon ground black pepper

PARSNIPS

4 parsnips, peeled and cut into thin strips 2 inches (5 cm) long and ¼ inch (6 mm) wide

¾ cup (6 fl oz/190 ml) water

salt and ground black pepper

¼ cup (2 oz/60 g) unsalted butter

2 tablespoons chopped fresh parsley

❖ For the short ribs, heat the olive oil in a large saucepan over high heat. When the pan is hot, add the veal short ribs and fry for about 2 minutes on each side, or until browned all over. Using tongs, transfer the short ribs to a plate. Set aside.

❖ To the same saucepan, over medium heat, add the carrots, onion, celery, and garlic, and cook for about 5 minutes, or until they begin to brown.

❖ Pour the wine into the pan and deglaze by stirring to dislodge any browned bits from the bottom of the pan. Bring to the boil and return the short ribs to the pan. Add the stock, bouquet garni, salt, and pepper, and return to the boil. Reduce the heat to medium–low and simmer for about 1 hour, or until the meat pulls easily away from the bones.

❖ Meanwhile, combine the parsnips, water, and salt and pepper to taste in a large frying pan over high heat. Bring to the boil and cook for about 5 minutes, or until the liquid has evaporated and the parsnips are tender. Add the butter and cook for 3–4 minutes, or until the parsnips are golden brown.

❖ Once the meat and vegetables are done, use tongs to transfer the short ribs to a warmed platter. Strain some of the pan juices through a fine-mesh sieve directly over the ribs. Arrange the parsnips alongside the meat, sprinkle the parsley over the ribs and parsnips, and serve.

cassoulet

serves 8–10

duck leg confit (page 215)

4½ cups (2 lb/1 kg) dried white beans

1 white onion

5 whole cloves

½ cup (4 oz/125 g) rendered duck fat,
from preparing the confit

1 carrot, peeled and coarsely chopped

2 ribs (sticks) celery, coarsely chopped

⅔ cup (3 oz/100 g) cloves garlic
(about 2 heads)

1 piece pancetta (½ lb/250 g),
cut into 1-inch (2.5-cm) cubes

10 cups (2½ qt/2.5 l) veal stock

2 cups (16 fl oz/500 ml) water

½ lb (250 g) smoked ham hock

2 tomatoes, cut into fourths

bouquet garni (see Glossary, page 310)

½ teaspoon salt

1 tablespoon whole black peppercorns

2 lb (1 kg) boneless lamb shoulder

2 tablespoons olive oil

1 cup (8 fl oz/250 ml) dry white wine

1 lb (500 g) cooked pork sausage, cut
in half lengthwise

½ cup (2 oz/60 g) fine dried bread crumbs

✥ Prepare the duck leg confit; set aside.

✥ Sort through the beans, discarding any grit or misshapen beans. Place beans in a large bowl, add water to cover generously, and let soak overnight. Drain the beans and rinse well; set aside.

✥ Cut the onion in half and chop half of it. Stud the other half with the 5 cloves.

✥ Heat the rendered fat in a large, heavy-bottomed saucepan or stockpot over high heat. Add the carrot, celery, chopped onion, garlic, and pancetta, and cook for about 5 minutes, or until the vegetables start to brown.

✥ Add the white beans, 8 cups (64 fl oz/2 l) of the veal stock, the water, clove-studded onion, ham hock, tomatoes, bouquet garni, salt, and peppercorns. Bring to a boil. Reduce the heat to medium, cover, and simmer for about 1 hour, or until beans are tender but not mushy.

✥ Meanwhile, trim any excess fat from the lamb shoulder and cut the meat into 1-inch (2.5-cm) cubes. Heat the olive oil in a large frying pan over high heat. Add the lamb and cook, in batches, for about 5 minutes, or until the meat begins to brown. Using a slotted spoon, transfer the meat to a plate and set aside.

✥ Pour off the fat from the pan and return the pan to high heat. When the pan is hot, pour in the wine and deglaze by stirring to dislodge any browned bits from the bottom of the pan. Return the lamb to the pan, add the remaining 2 cups (16 fl oz/500 ml) veal stock, and bring to the boil. Reduce the heat to medium and simmer for about 45 minutes, or until the lamb is

cassoulet

Cassoulet originated in the Languedoc region of southwest France. The main ingredient is always white beans, to which are added a variety of different meats according to the region. This one, combining lamb with sausage and duck confit, is similar to the classic cassoulets of Toulouse.

tender when pierced with a fork. Remove and discard the clove-studded onion and bouquet garni.

✥ Preheat the oven to 400°F (200°C/Gas Mark 5).

✥ Remove the duck legs from the fat and place on a rack in a baking pan; reserve the rendered fat for other uses. Heat the duck legs in the oven for 2–3 minutes, or until all the fat melts off.

✥ Add the duck legs, lamb shoulder, and sausage to the beans. Bring to the boil and simmer, stirring gently, to blend the flavors, for about 3 minutes.

✥ Transfer the contents of the pot to a large, heavy-bottomed baking dish. Distribute the meats evenly and sprinkle the bread crumbs evenly over the top. Bake in the oven for about 20 minutes, or until nicely browned on top. Serve immediately.

lamb stew
with artichokes

serves 4

While artichokes are the classic choice for this dill-scented stew, you could replace them with celery, fennel, or carrots. The last-minute avgolemono-style thickening with egg and lemon is an added flourish that truly pulls the dish together. The stew can be prepared a day or two ahead; add the eggs during the reheating.

3–4 tablespoons olive oil

2½ lb (1.25 kg) boneless lamb shoulder, trimmed of excess fat and cut into 2-inch (5-cm) pieces

3 onions, chopped

3 cloves garlic, chopped

1½ cups (12 fl oz/375 ml) water or chicken stock, or as needed

½ cup (4 fl oz/125 ml) fresh lemon juice

6 medium artichokes

2 lb (1 kg) assorted greens, such as romaine (cos) lettuce, dandelion greens, or Swiss chard (silverbeet), stemmed, well rinsed, drained, and torn into bite-size pieces (optional)

salt and ground black pepper

½ cup (½ oz/15 g) chopped fresh dill

2 eggs, at room temperature

lamb stew with artichokes

❖ Heat 2 tablespoons of olive oil in a large frying pan over high heat. Add the lamb and cook, in batches, for about 10 minutes, or until browned on all sides. Use a slotted spoon to transfer the browned lamb to a large, heavy pot.

❖ Add more olive oil, if needed, to the frying pan and cook the onions over medium heat for about 5 minutes, or until softened. Add the garlic and cook for 3 minutes longer. Transfer the contents of the frying pan to the pot containing the lamb. Increase the heat to high, pour ½ cup (4 fl oz/125 ml) of the water or stock into the pan, and deglaze by stirring to dislodge any browned bits from the bottom of the pan. Add the pan juices to the lamb.

❖ Add the remaining 1 cup (8 fl oz/250 ml) water or stock to the pot, or as needed to cover the meat. Bring to the boil, reduce the heat to low, cover, and simmer for 45 minutes.

❖ Meanwhile, fill a large bowl three-fourths full with water and add half the lemon juice. Snap off the tough outer leaves from the artichokes. Using a paring knife, trim the dark green parts from the base and stem. Cut the artichokes lengthwise into fourths, then scoop out and discard the prickly chokes. As they are cut, drop the artichokes into the bowl of acidulated lemon water to prevent discoloring. Drain when needed.

lamb stew with artichokes

◈ If using the greens, fill a large saucepan three-fourths full with water and bring to the boil. Add salt to taste and then the greens. Boil until tender, about 10 minutes, then drain well.

◈ When the lamb has simmered for 45 minutes, drain the artichokes and add them to the pot along with the greens. Continue to simmer for about 20 minutes longer, or until the lamb and artichokes are tender.

◈ Add the dill and season to taste with salt and pepper. Simmer for 5 minutes. At the last minute, beat the eggs in a bowl until very frothy. Gradually beat in the remaining lemon juice. Then gradually beat in about 1 cup (8 fl oz/250 ml) of the hot lamb juices, beating constantly to prevent curdling. Slowly stir the egg mixture into the hot stew. Heat through but do not allow the stew to boil.

◈ Transfer to a warmed serving dish and serve hot.

veal and wine terrine

serves 6

This recipe is best made two days ahead so the flavors have time to develop fully.

¼ cup (2 oz/60 g) butter, melted

2 lb (1 kg) bacon slices (rashers), rind removed

2 cups (2 oz/60 g) chopped parsley

1 cup (1 oz/30 g) chopped fresh chives

1 cup (1 oz/30 g) chopped fresh basil

3 tablespoons chopped fresh sage

2 tablespoons chopped fresh tarragon

3 onions, chopped

1½ lb (750 g) veal cutlets, thinly sliced

½ cup (4 fl oz/125 ml) dry white wine

✤ Preheat oven to 350°F (180°C/Gas Mark 4).

✤ Line the base and sides of a 9- x 5-inch (22- x 12-cm) terrine or loaf pan with foil, making sure the foil overlaps the sides. Brush the foil with butter and arrange the bacon to completely cover the base and sides of the terrine (the ends should hang over the sides; they will be tucked in later).

✤ Combine the herbs and onions.

✤ Arrange slices of veal on top of the bacon, making sure the bacon is completely covered. Spoon about one-fourth of the herb mixture evenly onto the veal. Place a layer of bacon lengthwise along the top of the herb mixture. Keep layering the ingredients until all are used, finishing the terrine with a layer of veal.

✤ Pour wine into the terrine and wait for about 5 minutes, or until it is absorbed. Bring the bacon overhanging the sides across the top of the terrine to seal. Cover terrine with foil and place in a baking dish. Pour water into the baking dish to come halfway up the sides of the terrine. Bake for about 1½ hours, or until cooked through. Remove from the oven and allow to cool. When completely cold, place a weight on the terrine and refrigerate overnight.

✤ To serve, turn out the terrine, remove the foil, and slice.

seafood and okra gumbo

serves 8–10

1/3 cup (3 fl oz/90 ml) vegetable oil

1 yellow onion, coarsely chopped

2 cloves garlic, finely chopped

3 tablespoons all-purpose (plain) flour

4 cups (1 qt/1 liter) fish stock, heated

1 can (16 oz/500 g) plum (Roma) tomatoes
with their juice

1 lb (500 g) cooked crabmeat,
coarsely flaked

1/2 lb (250 g) okra, trimmed and cut
into 1/2-inch (1-cm) pieces

1 green bell pepper (capsicum),
seeds and ribs removed, diced

2 bay leaves

1 teaspoon each dried basil,
dried oregano, and dried thyme

1–2 teaspoons hot-pepper sauce,
plus extra for serving

salt and ground pepper

1 lb (500 g) shrimp (prawns),
peeled and deveined

2 cups (14 oz/440 g) long-grain white
rice, steamed

Heat the oil in a large, heavy saucepan over low to medium heat. Add the onion and garlic and cook for 2–3 minutes, or until translucent. Reduce the heat to low, sprinkle in the flour, and continue to cook, stirring occasionally, for about 5 minutes more, or until the flour turns hazelnut brown. Whisking continuously, slowly stir in the stock.

Add the tomatoes and their juice, crushing them slightly with a wooden spoon. Add the crabmeat, okra, bell pepper, bay leaves, basil, oregano, thyme, and hot-pepper sauce. Increase the heat and bring to the boil. Reduce the heat to low, partly cover, and simmer for about 1 hour, or until thick but still fairly liquid.

Season to taste with salt, pepper and, if you like, more hot-pepper sauce. Stir in the shrimp and simmer for about 5 minutes, or until pink and cooked through. Mound some of the rice in the center of individual soup bowls and ladle the gumbo over it. Pass the extra hot-pepper sauce separately.

recipe hint

You can make a meal of this hearty soup from Louisiana, U.S.A. If you like, add chicken, diced ham, or andouille sausage with the crabmeat.

chicken casserole
with buttermilk dumplings

serves 4–6

1 chicken, 3 lb (1.5 kg), cut into 8 pieces

¼ cup (1½ oz/45 g) all-purpose (plain) flour

2 tablespoons olive oil

3 tablespoons butter

1 large yellow onion, chopped

½ red bell pepper (capsicum), seeded and chopped

4 oz (125 g) mushrooms, thickly sliced

1½ cups (12 fl oz/375 ml) chicken stock

1 carrot, cut into thin batons 2 inches (5 cm) long

2 ribs (sticks) celery, cut into thin batons 2 inches (5 cm) long

salt and ground black pepper

¾ cup (3½ oz/100 g) frozen or fresh peas

BUTTERMILK DUMPLINGS

1 cup (5 oz/150 g) all-purpose (plain) flour

2 teaspoons baking powder

½ cup (½ oz/15 g) chopped parsley

½ cup (4 fl oz/125 ml) buttermilk

✧ Pat the chicken pieces dry with paper towels. Place the flour in a plastic bag, add the chicken, and shake to coat evenly with the flour. Reserve the excess flour.

✧ Heat half the oil and half the butter in a large frying pan and cook half the chicken, turning once, for 3–4 minutes, or until the chicken pieces are golden brown. Place in the slow cooker. Repeat with the remaining oil, butter, and chicken pieces.

✧ Add the chopped onion, bell pepper, and mushrooms to the frying pan, and cook, stirring, for 2–3 minutes, or until lightly browned. Sprinkle on the reserved flour and add the chicken stock. Mix well.

✧ Pour the mixture over the chicken pieces in the slow cooker. Scatter the carrot and celery batons around the chicken and season to taste. Put on the lid and cook on Low for 7–9 hours.

✧ Remove lid for the last hour of cooking, and stir in the peas. Add the dumplings at this point.

✧ For the buttermilk dumplings, sift the flour and baking powder into a medium bowl. Stir in the parsley. Make a well in the center and mix in the buttermilk with a fork until just blended. Add a little more buttermilk or water, if necessary, to make a moist batter.

✧ Drop 6 spoonfuls of the dumpling mixture evenly around the chicken. Cook, uncovered, for 30 minutes. Cover and cook for 30 minutes more, or until the dumplings are firm (a toothpick inserted in the center should come out clean).

✧ Serve at once on warmed plates.

braised pork with quinces

serves 6

Quinces are prized in Greece and Turkey during the fall months, when their unique scent perfumes every kitchen. If you cannot find quinces, substitute apples or pears and reduce the sugar to 2 tablespoons. Although pork is naturally sweet and a wonderful foil for quince, this stew can also be made with beef or lamb.

2½ lb (1.25 kg) boneless pork shoulder, trimmed of excess fat and cut into 2-inch (5-cm) cubes

2 teaspoons ground cinnamon

2 teaspoons ground cumin

juice of 1 lemon

3 lb (1.5 kg) quinces

2 tablespoons (1 oz/30 g) unsalted butter

½ cup (4 oz/125 g) sugar

1 cup (8 fl oz/250 ml) pomegranate juice or water

¼ cup (2 fl oz/60 ml) olive oil

2 onions, chopped

pinch of ground cayenne pepper (optional)

1 cup (8 fl oz/250 ml) chicken stock or water

salt and ground black pepper

❖ Rub the meat with half the cinnamon and half the cumin and place in a nonreactive bowl. Cover and let marinate for 2 hours at room temperature, or overnight in the refrigerator.

❖ Fill a large bowl three-fourths full with water and add the lemon juice. Peel, core, and slice the quinces thickly. As they are cut, drop them into the lemon water to prevent discoloration.

❖ Drain the quince slices and pat dry with paper towels. Melt the butter in a frying pan over medium heat and cook the quinces for about 10 minutes, or until softened. Sprinkle with the sugar and continue to cook over low heat for 15–20 minutes more, or until golden. Add the pomegranate juice or water and simmer over low heat for 15–20 minutes longer, or until tender. Remove from the heat and let stand for 1 hour; or cool, cover, and let stand overnight.

❖ Heat the oil in a large, heavy frying pan over medium heat. Add the pork and cook for about 10 minutes, or until browned on all sides. Using a slotted spoon, transfer the pork to a plate; set aside.

❖ Add the onions to the fat remaining in the pan and cook over medium heat for about 8 minutes, or until tender. Add the remaining cinnamon and cumin, and the cayenne, if using, and cook for a few minutes longer to blend the flavors. Return the meat to the pan. Add the stock or water and stir well. Reduce the heat to low, cover, and simmer for 1 hour.

❖ Reheat the quinces over medium heat and add them and their juice to the meat. Simmer for about 30 minutes longer, or until the meat is tender and the flavors have blended. Season to taste with salt and pepper.

❖ Spoon the stew into a warmed serving dish and serve hot.

roast leg of
lamb
with yogurt

serves 6

While yogurt is more commonly used as a tenderizing marinade for lamb kabobs, in this recipe from Crete it is mixed with cinnamon and spread on a leg of lamb during only the last 15 minutes of roasting. Surprisingly, the yogurt forms a wonderful savory crust.

1 leg of lamb on the bone, 5–6 lb (2.5–3 kg)

6 cloves garlic, plus 2 teaspoons chopped garlic

2 teaspoons plus 3 tablespoons chopped fresh rosemary

5 tablespoons (2 1/2 fl oz/75 ml) olive oil

4 tablespoons (2 fl oz/60 ml) fresh lemon juice

salt and ground pepper

1 1/2 cups (12 oz/375 g) whole-milk or lowfat plain yogurt

1 teaspoon ground cinnamon

1/2 teaspoon all-purpose (plain) flour

❖ Using a small, sharp knife, cut about 12 slits, each about ½ inch (1 cm) deep, in the leg of lamb, spacing them evenly. Cut 3 of the garlic cloves into thin slivers and place in a small bowl with the 2 teaspoons rosemary. Mix well and insert the garlic mixture in the slits.

❖ Finely chop the remaining 3 garlic cloves and place in a small bowl. Add 2 tablespoons of the rosemary, 2 tablespoons of the olive oil, and 2 tablespoons of the lemon juice and mix well. Rub this mixture all over the leg of lamb. Cover and let marinate for 2 hours at room temperature or overnight in the refrigerator.

❖ Preheat the oven to 350°F (180°C/Gas Mark 4).

❖ Place the lamb in a roasting pan and sprinkle with salt and pepper.

❖ Whisk the remaining 3 tablespoons olive oil with the remaining 2 tablespoons lemon juice in a small bowl. Add the remaining 1 tablespoon rosemary and the 2 teaspoons chopped garlic. Roast the lamb, basting every 20 minutes with the oil-lemon mixture, for 1¼ hours.

❖ Whisk the yogurt with the cinnamon and flour in another bowl. Spoon the mixture over the lamb and continue to roast for about 15 minutes longer for medium-rare, or until the lamb is done to your liking and the yogurt sauce forms a crust. To test, insert an instant-read thermometer into the thickest part of the leg away from the bone; it should register 125°F (52°C) for medium-rare. Transfer the lamb to a warmed serving platter and leave to rest in a warm place for 8–10 minutes before carving. Serve hot.

tourtière

PASTRY

2 cups (10 oz/315 g) all-purpose
(plain) flour

½ teaspoon baking powder

½ teaspoon dried thyme, crushed

¼ teaspoon salt

⅔ cup (5 oz/150 g) shortening or butter

1 egg, beaten

2 tablespoons cold water

1 teaspoon lemon juice

FILLING

1 lb (500 g) ground (minced) pork

1 large carrot, coarsely shredded
(about 1 cup/5 oz/150 g)

1 small onion, chopped

2 slices (rashers) bacon, rind removed,
finely chopped

2 medium potatoes, peeled and chopped

¾ cup (6 fl oz/190 ml) beef stock

2 cloves garlic, chopped

1 teaspoon dried sage, crushed

½ teaspoon salt

¼ teaspoon pepper

For the pastry, combine the flour, baking powder, thyme, and salt. Cut in the shortening or butter until the pieces are the size of small peas. Set aside. Mix the egg, cold water, and lemon juice, and sprinkle over the flour mixture, 1 tablespoon at a time, tossing gently with a fork. Divide the mixture in halves. Shape each half into a ball and chill for at least 30 minutes.

Cook the pork, carrot, onion, and bacon in a large frying pan until pork is browned and onion is tender. Drain off the fat. Combine potatoes, stock, and garlic in a medium saucepan and bring to the boil. Reduce heat and simmer, covered, for about 10 minutes, or until potatoes are tender. Do not drain. Mash potato mixture and stir in pork mixture, sage, salt, and pepper.

Preheat the oven to 400°F (200°C/Gas Mark 5). Roll out the pastry and line a 9-inch (23-cm) pie plate with one sheet. Pile the filling in the pastry shell. Cut slits in the second pastry sheet and place over the filling. Trim, seal, and crimp edge of pastry. Bake for 25–30 minutes, or until golden brown. Let rest for 10 minutes.

recipe hint

Tourtière is a classic Canadian pork pie, often served on Christmas Eve. Its savory crust, seasoned with thyme, would also be good with your favorite chicken or beef pie filling.

asparagus and ham
lasagne rolls

This is an attractive way to present asparagus spears when they are at their best and most flavorsome. Serve two rolls per person as a main course, or one per person as an appetizer.

serves 4

1 sheet (about 1 lb/500 g) fresh pasta, cut into 8 equal squares

13 oz (400 g) fresh asparagus

1 cup (3½ oz/100 g) freshly grated Parmesan cheese

8 slices (13 oz/400 g) cooked ham

BÉCHAMEL SAUCE

3½ oz (100 g) butter

3 tablespoons all-purpose (plain) flour

1½ cups (12 fl oz/375 ml) milk

½ cup (4 fl oz/125 ml) dry white wine

½ cup (4 fl oz/125 ml) light (single) cream

❀ Bring a large pot of water to the boil. Drop in the pasta squares, one or two at a time, and cook for 2–3 minutes, or until they are just tender. Remove the pasta squares from the water and drain on clean tea towels.

❀ Cook the asparagus in boiling water until just tender. Drain, refresh under cold water, and drain again.

❀ For the béchamel sauce, melt the butter in a saucepan, add the flour, and stir to form a roux. Cook gently for 1–2 minutes. Remove saucepan from heat and gradually stir in the milk, then the wine. Return the saucepan to the heat and cook, stirring constantly, until the mixture boils and thickens. Stir in the cream and warm through, without boiling. Cover and set aside.

❀ Preheat the oven to 350°F (180°C/Gas Mark 4).

❀ For the rolls, lay out the pasta squares and spread 1 tablespoon of béchamel sauce over each. Sprinkle each with 1 tablespoon grated Parmesan. Top each sheet with 1 slice ham and 3–4 spears of asparagus. Roll up the sheets and secure with a toothpick, if necessary. Place the rolls side by side in a greased ceramic baking dish. Pour on the remaining béchamel sauce, ensuring that each roll is well coated. Sprinkle with the remaining Parmesan.

❀ Bake, uncovered, for about 30 minutes, or until the top is golden and bubbling. Serve hot.

spaghetti
with braised pork ribs

serves 6

2½ lb (1.25 kg) meaty pork spareribs

3 tablespoons olive or vegetable oil

1 large onion, chopped

3 cloves garlic, chopped

1 can (14 oz/440 g) crushed tomatoes

1½ cups (12 fl oz/375 ml) water

1 cinnamon stick

1 bay leaf

1 whole clove

½–1 teaspoon paprika

salt and ground black pepper

3 tablespoons finely chopped parsley

1½ lb (750 g) dried spaghetti

⅓ cup (¾ oz/20 g) pitted black olives

finely grated Parmesan cheese (optional)

❖ Preheat the oven to 350°F (180°C/Gas Mark 4).

❖ Place the ribs in a casserole. Heat two-thirds of the oil in a frying pan and cook the onion and garlic until lightly colored. Add the tomatoes and water and bring to the boil. Pour over the ribs and add the cinnamon stick, bay leaf, and clove. Cover and bake for 2 hours, or until the ribs are very tender.

❖ Remove the meat and cut into small cubes. Transfer the liquid to a saucepan and add the paprika, salt and pepper to taste, and half the parsley. Boil rapidly until reduced to about 3 cups (24 fl oz/750 ml). Add the meat from the ribs and keep warm.

❖ Bring a large pan of salted water to the boil and add the remaining oil and the pasta. Bring just to the boil, then cook with the water barely simmering for about 12 minutes, or until the pasta is tender. Transfer the pasta to a colander to drain, then place in a large serving dish and pour the meat and sauce over, or serve in deep bowls. Garnish with the olives, Parmesan, and the remaining parsley.

stuffed turkey breast roll

serves 6–8

This dish can be assembled in advance, wrapped in aluminum foil, and refrigerated for up to 1 day before cooking.

The uncooked roll can also be frozen. To serve, bake in the oven for about 1½ hours.

1 small boneless turkey breast, about 3 lb (1.5 kg)

1 cup (5 oz/155 g) green peas

1 lb (500 g) pork or spicy pork sausages

2 teaspoons butter or vegetable oil

1 small onion, finely chopped

1 slice (rasher) bacon, rind removed, finely diced

2 tablespoons finely chopped red bell pepper (capsicum) or canned pimiento

1 teaspoon dried mixed herbs

1 teaspoon chopped parsley

¼ teaspoon ground sage

salt and ground black pepper

✥ Preheat the oven to 375°F (190°C/Gas Mark 4).

✥ Place the turkey breast, skin side down, on a worktop and trim the thicker parts of meat, transferring them to areas where the meat is thinner, to give an even thickness of meat. The spread breast should be about 14 x 11 inches (35 x 28 cm) in size.

✥ Boil the peas in lightly salted water and drain well. Slit open the sausages to extract the meat and place in a mixing bowl. Discard the sausage casings. Heat the butter or oil in a small frying pan and cook the onion and bacon until lightly colored. If using the bell pepper, add it now and fry briefly (canned pimiento does not require cooking). Mix with the pork, peas, mixed herbs, parsley, and sage. Season generously with salt and pepper. Spread over the turkey breast and roll up.

✥ Use fine clean string to tie the roll at ¾-inch (2-cm) intervals. Rub the surface with butter or oil and sprinkle with salt and pepper. Place, seam side down, in a baking dish just large enough to hold the roll, and roast for about 1 hour. Test with a meat thermometer after 45 minutes, and cook for the required extra time, if needed (the internal temperature of the roll should reach 185°F/85°C). Remove from the oven and let rest for 10 minutes. Cut into thick slices to serve hot with vegetables, or allow to cool completely and slice thinly to serve cold with a salad.

marinated
barbecued
leg of lamb

serves 6

1 leg of lamb, about 6 lb (3 kg)

4–6 cloves garlic, peeled and slivered

3 tablespoons vegetable oil or melted butter

cracked black pepper

MARINADE

2 tablespoons red wine vinegar

2 cups (16 fl oz/500 ml) dry white or red wine

1 teaspoon black peppercorns

4 bay leaves

1 teaspoon juniper berries

2 sprigs fresh parsley

1 medium onion, chopped

1 small carrot, chopped

1 teaspoon salt

❖ Trim any excess fat from the leg. Remove the lamb bone by cutting the length of the leg on the thinnest side where the bone is close to the surface. Use a small sharp knife to work around the bone until it can be removed (or ask your butcher to bone the leg). Pierce the meat with a sharp knife evenly over the whole piece and insert the garlic slivers in the slits.

❖ Combine marinade ingredients in a large bowl and add the lamb. Cover with plastic wrap and refrigerate for 24 hours, turning several times. Drain well.

❖ Pat the surface of the lamb dry with paper towels and rub with oil or melted butter. Season with pepper.

❖ Preheat a grill (barbecue) to medium heat and brush the meat with oil. Cook the lamb for 45–60 minutes, or until the surface is well crisped and the meat just cooked through. Turn several times during cooking, basting each time with extra oil or butter. Remove from the heat and let rest for 5–10 minutes.

❖ Slice and serve with salads or potatoes baked in foil.

recipe hint

Use tongs to turn the lamb on the barbecue. If you pierce the flesh with a fork once it is sealed, you will lose the delicious juices that keep the meat from becoming dry.

mustard beef
with horseradish mayonnaise

serves 10–12

2 scotch fillets, 3 lb (1.5 kg) each

2 cups (16 fl oz/500 ml) red wine

½ cup (4 fl oz/125 ml) oil

2 cloves garlic, crushed

2 bay leaves

1 onion, peeled and chopped

cracked black peppercorns

HORSERADISH MAYONNAISE

¼ cup (2 oz/60 g) butter, melted

¾ cup (6 fl oz/185 ml) mayonnaise

2 tablespoons sour cream

2 tablespoons horseradish cream

1 tablespoon Dijon mustard

2 tablespoons white wine vinegar

½ cup (½ oz/15 g) chopped chives

❖ Preheat the oven to 350°F (180°C/Gas Mark 4).

❖ Tie the beef fillets together, top to tail, with string and place in a shallow dish. Add the red wine, oil, garlic, bay leaves, and onion, and marinate for several hours. Pour off 2 cups (16 fl oz/500 ml) of the marinade and discard. Roast the beef with the remaining marinade for about 1¼ hours, or until cooked as desired. Cool to room temperature, remove the string, and roll the meat in the cracked peppercorns.

❖ Combine all mayonnaise ingredients in a bowl and mix well. Serve the beef warm or at room temperature. Slice, arrange on a platter, and pass the mayonnaise separately.

spicy chicken and beans

serves 6

1 tablespoon vegetable oil

1 medium yellow onion, chopped

2 ribs (sticks) celery, finely chopped

2 cloves garlic, chopped

1 tablespoon chili powder

1 teaspoon ground cumin

1 teaspoon dried oregano leaves

1 lb (500 g) ground (minced) chicken meat

1 can (14 oz/440 g) tomato pasta sauce

1 can (14 oz/440 g) tomatoes, chopped

1 can (4 oz/125 g) mild green chiles, rinsed and drained

1 can (14 oz/440 g) pinto beans, rinsed and drained

salt and ground black pepper

½ cup (¾ oz/25 g) chopped fresh cilantro (coriander)

sour cream, to serve

❖ Heat the oil in a large frying pan and cook the onion, celery, and garlic for 2–3 minutes, or until softened. Stir in the chili powder, cumin, and oregano leaves, and cook for 1 minute more.

❖ Increase the heat and add the chicken meat, stirring and mashing it with a fork until it has changed color.

❖ Stir in tomato sauce, tomatoes, chiles, and beans, and season to taste. Transfer to the slow cooker. Put on the lid and cook on Low for 6–8 hours.

❖ To serve, sprinkle with cilantro and top with sour cream.

barbecued
stuffed leg of lamb

serves 6

The boned leg can be prepared in advance, stuffed, rolled, and tied. The stuffed and prepared leg can also be frozen, uncooked. Defrost slowly before cooking as directed in the recipe.

1 leg of lamb, about 5 lb (2.5 kg)

salt and ground black pepper

6 oz (185 g) ground (minced) pork

6 oz (185 g) ground (minced) veal

4 oz (125 g) cooked ham, finely ground (minced)

4 oz (125 g) chicken livers, very finely chopped, or pâté

2 tablespoons (1 oz/30 g) butter

1 small onion, finely chopped

3 oz (100 g) fresh mushrooms, finely chopped

1 teaspoon dried mixed Provençal or Italian herbs

extra butter or oil

10 small sprigs rosemary

2 cloves garlic, slivered

✥ Preheat a kettle barbecue to medium, or preheat the oven to 350°F (180°C/Gas Mark 4).

✥ Remove the lamb bone by cutting the length of the leg on the thinnest side where the bone is close to the surface. Use a small sharp knife to work around the bone until it can be removed (or ask your butcher to bone the leg). Season the inside surface with salt and pepper.

✥ Mix the ground meats with the ham and chicken liver or pâté. Heat the butter in a frying pan and cook the onion until slightly softened and lightly colored. Add the mushrooms and cook for 2–3 minutes. Add the dried herbs, salt, and pepper, and mix the contents of the pan with the meats. Knead the stuffing to amalgamate the ingredients well.

✥ Spread the stuffing over the inside of the leg and fold the meat around the stuffing, forming it back into its original shape. Tie securely at close intervals with kitchen string. Rub with salt and pepper, pierce in several places with a sharp knife, and insert a small sprig of rosemary and a sliver of garlic in each slit. Roast in the barbecue (or the oven) for about 1½ hours, or until cooked through. Baste the meat from time to time during cooking with its own juices. Remove and allow to rest in a warm place for 10 minutes before slicing to serve.

creamy chicken and leek pie

serves 6–8

2 cups (10 oz/315 g) all-purpose (plain) flour

2/3 cup (5 oz/150 g) cream cheese, chopped

1/3 cup (3 oz/90 g) butter, chopped

3 egg yolks

about 1 tablespoon water, plus 2 teaspoons extra

FILLING

1 tablespoon vegetable oil

1 1/2 lb (750 g) boneless, skinless chicken breasts, chopped

2 leeks, sliced and well washed

3 bacon strips (rashers), rind removed, chopped

2 cloves garlic, crushed

3 tablespoons (1 1/2 oz/45 g) butter

2 tablespoons all-purpose (plain) flour

1/2 cup (4 fl oz/125 ml) dry white wine

1 cup (8 fl oz/250 ml) milk

1/3 cup (2 oz/60 g) shredded Cheddar cheese

1/3 cup (1 oz/30 g) grated Parmesan cheese

2 teaspoons grain mustard

1 tablespoon chopped fresh thyme

salt and ground black pepper

❖ Lightly grease a 9–10-inch (23–25-cm) pie dish.

❖ Sift the flour into a bowl; rub in the cream cheese and butter. Add 2 egg yolks and about 1 tablespoon water, or enough to make the ingredients cling together. (This can be done in a food processor.) Knead pastry dough gently until smooth, cover and refrigerate for 30 minutes.

❖ Preheat the oven to 400°F (200°C/Gas Mark 5). Divide the dough in halves and roll one half out to line the bottom and sides of the pie dish. Trim the edge. Cover the pastry with foil or parchment (baking) paper, and fill with dried beans. Bake for 15 minutes. Remove paper and beans and bake for a further 10 minutes, or until pastry is lightly browned. Leave to cool.

❖ Meanwhile, for the filling, heat the oil in a frying pan and cook the chicken in batches, stirring, until browned. Remove from the pan. Reheat the pan and cook the leeks, bacon, and garlic, stirring, until the leeks are soft. Add the butter and flour and cook, stirring, until the liquid is bubbling. Remove from the heat and gradually add the wine and milk. Return to the heat and cook, stirring, until the mixture boils and thickens. Stir in the cheeses, mustard, thyme, and chicken; mix well and season to taste with salt and pepper. Cool slightly.

❖ Spoon filling into the pastry shell. Combine remaining egg yolk with 1½ teaspoons of water; brush on the edge of the pastry shell. Roll out the second half of the dough until it is large enough to cover the top of the pie. Lay the pastry over the filling and press the edges together firmly; trim and pinch the edge to decorate. Brush the pastry with more egg yolk mixture and decorate with pastry leaves cut from the pastry scraps. Cut two slits in the top pastry crust. Bake at 400°F (200°C/Gas Mark 5) for about 35 minutes, or until the pie is golden brown.

chicken
with couscous,
chickpeas, and cumin sauce

serves 4–6

COUSCOUS

2 cups (12 oz/375 g) couscous
(see Glossary, page 311)

1½ cups (12 fl oz/375 ml) boiling water

½ cup (4 oz/125 g) butter

1 onion, chopped

2 cloves garlic, crushed

2 teaspoons cumin seeds

2 teaspoons coriander seeds

1 teaspoon chopped fresh chile

½ teaspoon ground cinnamon

pinch of saffron

2 tablespoons currants

1 can (13 oz/400 g) chickpeas
(garbanzo beans), rinsed and drained

CHICKEN

1 chicken, about 3½ lb (1.8 kg)

2 tablespoons (1 oz/30 g) butter, melted

1 teaspoon ground cumin

2 teaspoons cumin seeds

2 cups (16 fl oz/500 ml) chicken stock

1 tablespoon plus 1 teaspoon honey

Harissa Sauce (page 159), to serve

✧ The couscous can be made a day ahead and reheated. Put couscous in a bowl and add the boiling water. Let stand for 2–3 minutes, or until the water is absorbed.

✧ Heat the butter in a frying pan and stir-fry the onion, garlic, cumin and coriander seeds, chile, and spices until the onion is soft. Add the couscous, currants, and chickpeas and cook, stirring, until well combined and heated through.

✧ Tie the chicken legs together and tuck the wings under the body. Place bird on a wire rack in a baking dish, brush with melted butter, and sprinkle with ground cumin. Pour ½ cup (4 fl oz/125 ml) water into the dish and bake at 350°F (180°C/Gas Mark 4) for about 1¾ hours, or until golden and tender.

✧ When the chicken is cooked, remove from the oven. Drain the fat from the dish and heat the remaining juices, stirring, until well browned. Add the cumin seeds and cook, stirring, until fragrant. Add the stock and honey and simmer for about 2 minutes, deglazing the pan by stirring to dislodge any browned bits from the bottom. Strain the sauce; serve with the chicken, couscous, and harissa sauce.

harissa sauce

8 oz (250 g) fresh chiles, seeded and chopped

1 head garlic, cloves peeled

1 tablespoon ground coriander

2 tablespoons each chopped fresh mint and cilantro (coriander) leaves

2 teaspoons salt

olive oil

✧ Process the combined ingredients or mash with a mortar and pestle, using enough olive oil to form a stiff paste, or the consistency you like. (To avoid skin burns, it is most important to wear gloves when seeding and chopping hot chiles.)

olive-seasoned chicken
with roasted vegetables

serves 4–6

The chicken can be prepared up to a day ahead but is best cooked close to serving.

If yellow pear (teardrop) tomatoes are unavailable, substitute red cherry tomatoes.

The chicken is also delicious served cold on bread rolls or for sandwiches.

1 chicken, about 3½ lb (1.8 kg)

⅓ cup (3 oz/90 g) butter, softened

½ cup (3½ oz/100 g) finely chopped pitted black olives

4 cloves garlic, crushed

ground black pepper

12 baby onions (about 10 oz/300 g), peeled

8 oz (250 g) red cherry tomatoes

8 oz (250 g) yellow pear (teardrop) tomatoes

½ cup (½ oz/15 g) lightly packed whole basil leaves

◈ Preheat the oven to 400°F (200°C/Gas Mark 5).

◈ Carefully loosen the chicken skin from over the breast.

◈ Beat the butter, olives, and garlic in a bowl with a wooden spoon until combined. Spoon the mixture under the skin of the chicken, and ease evenly over the flesh with your hands. Tie the chicken legs together and tuck the wings under the body. Sprinkle the chicken with pepper and roast in a baking dish for 45 minutes.

◈ Add the onions to the pan, turning them to coat in the pan juices; roast for a further 30 minutes. Add the tomatoes and basil and roast for a further 15 minutes, or until the chicken is tender.

◈ Remove the chicken from the oven and leave to rest for 5–10 minutes. Remove the string. Serve the chicken with the onions, tomatoes, and basil. Drizzle with some of the pan juices, if desired.

beef tamale
with cornmeal topping

serves 6–8

CORNMEAL TOPPING

4 cups (1 qt/1 liter) water

1 cup (5 oz/150 g) yellow cornmeal

1 cup (4 oz/125 g) shredded
Cheddar cheese

salt and ground black pepper

TAMALE

1 tablespoon vegetable oil

1 large yellow onion, chopped

½ green bell pepper (capsicum),
seeded and chopped

2 cloves garlic, finely chopped

1 tablespoon chili powder

½ teaspoon dried oregano leaves

1 lb (500 g) ground (minced) beef

1 can (28 oz/880 g) diced tomatoes

1 can (14 oz/440 g) kidney beans,
rinsed and drained

1½ cups (10 oz/300 g) fresh or
canned corn kernels

salt and ground black pepper

purchased hot or mild tomato salsa,
to serve

✥ For the cornmeal topping, bring the water to the boil in a large saucepan and slowly whisk in the cornmeal. Bring to the boil and simmer, stirring, for 5 minutes, or until thickened. Stir in the shredded Cheddar cheese. Season to taste with salt and pepper.

✥ For the beef tamale, heat the oil in a large frying pan and cook the onion, bell pepper, and garlic for 3 minutes, or until softened. Stir in the chili powder and oregano leaves, and cook for 1 minute more.

✥ Increase the heat and cook the beef, stirring and mashing with a fork until the meat has changed color.

✥ Stir in the diced tomatoes, kidney beans, and corn. Season to taste with salt and black pepper. Transfer to the slow cooker. Spread the cornmeal evenly over the beef mixture. Put on the lid and cook on Low for 6–8 hours. Serve hot with purchased tomato salsa.

recipe hint

No peeking while the food cooks in your slow cooker. When you remove the lid, the cooker can take up to 20 minutes to regain the correct temperature. If the recipe calls for the dish to be stirred, do this and replace the lid as quickly as possible to minimize the loss of heat.

wild rice stuffed chicken

with grand marnier glaze

serves 6

1 chicken, about 3½ lb (1.8 kg)

1 tablespoon orange marmalade

1 tablespoon Grand Marnier liqueur

STUFFING

½ cup (3½ oz/100 g) wild rice

1 tablespoon vegetable oil

1 onion, chopped

1 clove garlic, crushed

1 rib (stick) celery, chopped

¼ cup (¾ oz/20 g) chopped fresh chives

½ cup (½ oz/45 g) stale bread crumbs

½ cup (1¾ oz/50 g) chopped pecans

1 egg, lightly beaten

salt and ground black pepper

GRAND MARNIER GLAZE

¾ cup (6 fl oz/190 ml) dry white wine

¼ cup (2 oz/60 g) orange marmalade

1 tablespoon plus 1 teaspoon cornstarch (cornflour)

1 cup (8 fl oz/250 ml) orange juice

2 teaspoons Grand Marnier liqueur

❖ For the stuffing, cook the wild rice in a saucepan of boiling water, uncovered, for 20–30 minutes, or until the rice is just tender; drain.

❖ Heat the oil in a saucepan, and cook the onion, garlic, and celery, stirring, until the onion is soft; cool. Combine the wild rice and onion mixture with the remaining ingredients in a bowl and mix well.

❖ Preheat the oven to 400°F (200°C/Gas Mark 5).

❖ Fill the chicken cavity with the stuffing; tie the legs together and tuck the wings under the body. Place the chicken on a wire rack in a baking dish and pour ¼ cup (2 fl oz/60 ml) water into the dish. Roast, uncovered, for 1 hour.

❖ After an hour, brush the chicken with the combined marmalade and Grand Marnier and roast for a further 30 minutes, or until tender. The juices should run clear when the thigh is pierced in the thickest part with a skewer.

❖ For the glaze, combine the wine, marmalade, and cornstarch with one-fourth of the orange juice in a saucepan; stir until the mixture boils and thickens. Stir in the remaining orange juice and Grand Marnier and keep stirring until hot.

❖ When the chicken is cooked, let rest for 5–10 minutes in a warm place. Remove the string and serve with the sauce.

❖ The stuffing and glaze can be prepared a day ahead.

chicken curry

serves 4–6

This dish should be served with steamed rice and small bowls of lime wedges, chutney, chopped cucumber, spiced yogurt, grated coconut, nuts, and raisins.

1 chicken, about 3½ lb (1.8 kg)

2 tablespoons (1 oz/30 g) unsalted butter

4 green (spring) onions, chopped

3 tablespoons curry powder or garam masala

1 cup (8 fl oz/250 ml) coconut milk

2 cups (16 fl oz/500 ml) chicken stock

3 tablespoons chopped crystallized ginger

crushed dried chiles

2 teaspoons chopped fresh mint

2 tablespoons raisins

¼ cup (2 fl oz/60 ml) fresh lime juice

½ cup (4 fl oz/125 ml) heavy whipping (double) cream

sprigs of fresh mint, to garnish (optional)

❖ Put the chicken in a large saucepan with water to cover and bring just to the boil. Reduce the heat to as low as possible and simmer for 1 hour. (When poaching chicken, the water should be scarcely moving. Aromatic vegtables, such as onion, carrot, and celery, can be added to the water if you wish, and the poaching liquid can be used as the basis for stock.) Cool the chicken in the poaching liquid. When cold, remove the skin and bones, cut the meat into small chunks, and set aside.

❖ Heat the butter in a saucepan over medium heat and cook the onions for 2–3 minutes, or until soft. Stir in the curry powder or garam masala, mixing well with the onions and butter.

❖ Gradually add the coconut milk and half of the chicken stock. Bring to the boil, stirring to blend well.

❖ Reduce the heat and add the ginger, a tiny pinch of crushed dried chiles, and the mint. Cover and simmer for 30 minutes. Add the chicken pieces and the remaining stock and simmer for 15 minutes. Stir in the raisins, lime juice, and cream, and simmer for 5 minutes. Transfer to a warmed serving bowl and garnish with the mint sprigs, if desired.

chile pork with rice and beans

serves 6

1 tablespoon chili powder

1 teaspoon ground oregano

½ teaspoon ground cumin

salt and ground black pepper

2 lb (1 kg) boneless pork loin or shoulder, cut into 1-inch (2.5-cm) cubes

3 tablespoons vegetable oil

1 large sweet onion, finely chopped

½ red bell pepper (capsicum), seeded and finely chopped

3 cloves garlic, finely chopped

½ cup (3¼ oz/100 g) long-grain rice

1¼ cups (10 fl oz/315 ml) chicken stock

1 can (4 oz/125 g) green chiles, rinsed, drained, and diced

2 large tomatoes, seeded and chopped

1 can (15 oz/470 g) kidney beans, rinsed and drained

tortillas, to serve

fresh cilantro (coriander) leaves, to garnish

✧ Combine the spices and salt and pepper to taste in a large plastic bag. Add the pork cubes and shake to coat them thoroughly in the mixture.

✧ Heat half the oil in a large frying pan and cook the pork, stirring, over high heat until golden brown on all sides. Place the pork in the slow cooker.

✧ Heat the remaining oil in the frying pan, and cook the onion, bell pepper, and garlic, stirring, for 2–3 minutes, or until lightly golden. Stir in the rice, stock, green chiles, tomatoes, and kidney beans. Bring to the boil then pour over the pork in the slow cooker. Mix well to combine.

✧ Put on the lid and cook on Low for 8–10 hours. Serve hot with warmed tortillas, garnished with the fresh cilantro leaves.

recipe hint

Slow cooking tends to concentrate flavors, so be conservative when adding salt and other seasonings during the cooking time. You can always taste and add more just before serving, but if you've added too much, you can't take it out.

neapolitan-style braised beef
braciole

serves 4

A favorite dish in the trattorias of central and southern Italy, braciole consists of tender beef rolled around a filling of cheese and vegetables.

Open a good Chianti or similar robust red wine both for the cooking and to enjoy with the meal.

1 lb (500 g) top beef round, cut into 4 thin slices

4 thin slices (about ¼ lb/125 g) smoked baked ham

4 thin slices (about ¼ lb/125 g) Provolone cheese

2 tablespoons chopped fresh parsley

4 teaspoons chopped garlic

1 small carrot, peeled and chopped

4 teaspoons chopped celery, plus 2 tablespoons extra

3 tablespoons extra-virgin olive oil

¼ cup (1½ oz/45 g) chopped red (Spanish) onion

½ cup (4 fl oz/125 ml) Chianti or other Italian red wine, plus 2 tablespoons extra

2 cans (28 oz/880 g each) plum (Roma) tomatoes, drained and puréed

salt and ground pepper

✥ Place each beef slice between 2 sheets of plastic wrap and, using the flat side of a meat mallet, pound until about 1/8 inch (3 mm) thick. Place 1 ham slice on top of each beef slice, and top with a cheese slice.

✥ In a small bowl, combine the parsley, half the garlic, 1 tablespoon of the carrot, and the 4 teaspoons celery. Sprinkle the mixture evenly over the center of each cheese slice. Beginning at one end of each beef slice, roll up tightly and secure the seam with toothpicks. Seal the ends with toothpicks as well, to keep the filling from spilling out.

✥ Heat the olive oil in a deep saucepan over medium heat, and cook the beef rolls for 4–5 minutes, or until browned well on all sides. Reduce the heat to medium–low, add the remaining carrot, 2 tablespoons celery, and the onion and cook for 2 minutes. Add the remaining 2 teaspoons garlic and cook for 1–2 minutes, or until fragrant.

✥ Increase the heat to high, add the 1/2 cup (4 fl oz/125 ml) red wine, and deglaze the pan by stirring to dislodge the browned bits from the bottom of the pan. Boil for 1 minute, then add the puréed tomatoes. Return to a boil, then reduce the heat to low and simmer, uncovered, for about 1 1/2 hours, or until the beef rolls are tender when pierced with a fork.

✥ Add the remaining 2 tablespoons red wine and continue to simmer for 2 minutes longer. Season to taste with salt and pepper. Spoon onto warmed individual plates, remove the toothpicks, and serve immediately.

chicken
with garlic

serves 4

The garlic becomes soft and mild with roasting. Spread it instead of butter on thinly sliced warm bread and eat with the chicken.

Serve with mashed potatoes and zucchini (courgettes) grilled (barbecued) with their blossoms intact.

1 chicken, about 3½ lb (1.8 kg)

3 tablespoons unsalted butter, at room temperature

1 teaspoon dried sage

3 whole heads garlic, separated into cloves and peeled

6 green (spring) onions, including tender green tops, sliced lengthwise

½ cup (4 fl oz/125 ml) each dry white wine and chicken stock, or 1 cup (8 fl oz/250 ml) chicken stock

salt and ground black pepper

◈ Preheat the oven to 375°F (190°C/Gas Mark 4).

◈ Trim any excess fat from the chicken. Rub inside the cavity with 1 tablespoon of the butter and sprinkle with the sage. Place 8 of the garlic cloves inside. Rub 1 tablespoon of the butter on the bottom of a roasting pan. Scatter the green onions over the bottom and place the chicken on the bed of onions. Rub the entire surface of the chicken with the remaining 1 tablespoon butter. Place the bird on its side and tuck garlic cloves around the chicken and under the wings. Roast for 30 minutes.

◈ Turn the bird so it rests on its opposite side. Combine the wine, if using, and stock, and stir half of it into the pan. Baste the chicken and roast for another 30 minutes. Add the remaining stock mixture. Turn the chicken breast side up, baste with the pan juices, and season to taste with salt and pepper. Roast for another 20–30 minutes, or until the chicken is tender and golden. The juices should run clear when the thigh is pierced in the thickest part with a skewer.

◈ Transfer the chicken to a warmed platter with the garlic cloves. Carve at the table.

lemon chicken

serves 4

This golden chicken,
infused with the aroma
of lemon, is served on
a bed of watercress to
catch the delicious juices.
Roasted onions glazed
with balsamic vinegar
add a strong accent.

1 chicken, about 3½ lb (1.8 kg)

2 teaspoons dried tarragon

3 lemons

¼ cup (2 oz/60 g) unsalted butter

2 tablespoons Dijon mustard

4 yellow onions, cut in half crosswise

2 tablespoons balsamic vinegar

½ cup (4 fl oz/125 ml) chicken stock (broth)

salt and ground black pepper

1 bunch watercress

❖ Preheat the oven to 375°F (190°C/Gas Mark 4).

❖ Trim any excess fat from the chicken. Sprinkle inside the cavity with half the tarragon. Cut 1 lemon in half and place a lemon half in the cavity; truss the chicken.

❖ Squeeze the remaining lemons; you should have about ¼ cup (2 fl oz/60 ml) juice.

❖ Melt the butter in a small pan over medium heat. Stir in the lemon juice, the remaining tarragon, and the mustard, and mix well. Brush some of the butter mixture over the surface of the chicken. Place breast side down in a shallow roasting pan. Arrange the onions around the chicken and brush half of the remaining butter mixture over the onions. Roast for 30 minutes. Spoon the vinegar over the onions and stir the stock into the pan. Baste the chicken with the pan juices and roast for another 30 minutes.

❖ Turn the chicken breast side up, baste with the remaining butter mixture, and season with salt and pepper. Continue to roast for 20–30 minutes more, or until the chicken is tender and golden. The juices should run clear when the thigh is pierced in the thickest part with a skewer.

❖ Make a bed of watercress on a warmed platter. Place the bird on top and surround with the onions. Baste the chicken with some of the pan juices and serve the remaining juices in a small pitcher. Carve the chicken at the table.

lamb with new potatoes

serves 5–6

Although a roasted shoulder
of lamb is rather awkward
to carve, the meat on this
cut is sweet and succulent.
This recipe provides the
perfect way to enjoy the
delicate flavor of the
shoulder meat.

1 shoulder of lamb, about 2¾ lb (1.4 kg), boned and
trimmed, cut into 1-inch (2.5-cm) cubes

salt and ground black pepper

¼ cup (2 oz/60 g) butter

3½ oz (100 g) baby onions, chopped

1 potato, about 5 oz (155 g), finely grated

8 oz (250 g) baby carrots, sliced ⅛ inch (3 mm) thick

13 oz (410 g) very small new potatoes
(about 30 potatoes)

1 teaspoon balsamic vinegar

2 tablespoons chopped chervil

❖ Season the meat with salt and pepper.

❖ Melt the butter in a 16-cup (4-qt/4-l) pot. Add the meat and brown, turning constantly, over low heat for about 5 minutes, or until lightly browned. Transfer the meat to a bowl. Add the onions to the pot and cook, without browning, for 2 minutes. Add the grated potato and carrots. Return the lamb to the pot and add 2 cups (16 fl oz/500 ml) hot water. Cover the pot and cook for 1½ hours over very low heat.

❖ Meanwhile, peel the new potatoes, or scrape them if their skin is very fine.

❖ After the meat has cooked for 1½ hours, add the potatoes. Season with salt and pepper to taste. Cook for about 30 minutes more, or until the potatoes are very tender and can easily be pierced with a the point of a knife. Remove from the heat. Pour the vinegar into the pot and gently mix. Add the chervil and mix again.

❖ Spoon the lamb and baby potatoes into a deep dish and serve immediately.

rosemary chicken
with potatoes

serves 4

The chicken and potatoes absorb the rosemary's fragrance. Truss the chicken and tuck sprigs of fresh rosemary under the wings.

Serve with a green salad tossed with chopped celery, radishes, and chives. For a large dinner party, roast two birds together in a larger dish.

1 chicken, about 3½ lb (1.8 kg)

1 lemon, cut in half

6 sprigs fresh rosemary

4 Russet or baking potatoes, peeled and cut into 2-inch (5-cm) cubes

3 tablespoons (1½ oz/50 g) unsalted butter

3 tablespoons olive oil

2 teaspoons dried rosemary

1 teaspoon dried thyme

½ cup (4 fl oz/125 ml) chicken stock

salt and ground black pepper

❖ Preheat the oven to 350°F (180°C/Gas Mark 4).

❖ Trim any excess fat from the chicken. Rub inside and out with a lemon half. Place 2 rosemary sprigs in the cavity and tuck 1 rosemary sprig under each wing; truss the chicken securely.

❖ Place the chicken on its side in a roasting pan and surround with the potatoes.

❖ Melt the butter in a small pan and stir in the oil. Brush the butter mixture evenly over the chicken and potatoes and sprinkle with the dried rosemary and thyme.

❖ Roast for 30 minutes.

❖ Turn the chicken so it rests on its other side. Add the stock to the pan and baste the chicken with the pan juices. Roast for another 30 minutes.

❖ Turn the chicken breast side up, baste with the pan juices, and season to taste with salt and pepper. Roast for 20–30 minutes more, or until the chicken is tender.

❖ Transfer the chicken to a warmed platter and surround with the potatoes. Garnish with the remaining rosemary sprigs.

❖ Serve the pan juices separately in a small pitcher. Carve the chicken at the table.

sliced beef
in bell pepper sauce

serves 4

There's no need to buy an expensive piece of beef for this recipe. Slow cooking transforms cheaper, tougher cuts of meat, making them tender and palatable. Indeed, the flavor is often superior to that of cuts that are usually cooked more quickly.

2 onions, finely sliced

1 rib (stick) celery, cut into thin strips

1¾ lb (800 g) beef, sliced ¼ inch (6 mm) thick

salt and ground black pepper

1 bay leaf

juice of ½ lemon

1 sprig thyme

1 cup (8 fl oz/250 ml) dry red wine

1 tablespoon all-purpose (plain) flour

3 tablespoons extra-virgin olive oil

1 red bell pepper (capsicum), chopped

1 green bell pepper (capsicum), chopped

◈ Scatter the onions and celery over the bottom of a baking dish. Lay the beef slices on top and season to taste with salt and pepper. Add the bay leaf, lemon juice, and thyme leaves, and sprinkle on the wine.

◈ Cover the dish and marinate in the refrigerator for at least 2 hours.

◈ Drain the meat thoroughly and pat it dry with paper towels; strain the marinade, reserving the solids and liquid separately. Dredge the meat slices in flour. Heat the oil in a large frying pan, add the beef, and brown on both sides for about 5 minutes. Add the marinade liquid and let it evaporate a little before adding all the other marinade ingredients. Cook for a few minutes. Add the bell peppers, cover, and cook very slowly, on the lowest possible heat, or roast in a 275°F (135°C/Gas Mark 1) oven for about 2 hours, stirring from time to time.

◈ When the meat is well cooked, carefully remove the slices from the sauce and arrange them on a serving dish. Strain the sauce, pour it over the meat, and serve.

chicken and eggplant
casserole

serves 4–6

2 chickens, about 2½ lb (1.25 kg) each,
cut into fourths

3 tablespoons brandy (optional)

2 cloves garlic, cut in half

¼ cup (2 fl oz/60 ml) olive oil

salt and ground black pepper

2 cups (10 oz/315 g) chopped red and
yellow bell peppers (capsicums)

4 tomatoes, cut into fourths

1 small globe eggplant (aubergine), cut
lengthwise into strips

1 cup (8 fl oz/250 ml) chicken stock, heated,
and ½ cup (4 fl oz/125 ml) white wine, or
1½ cups (12 fl oz/375 ml) chicken stock

1 teaspoon dried thyme

2 bay leaves

1 tablespoon chopped fresh parsley

✧ Preheat the oven to 375°F (190°C/Gas Mark 4).

✧ Trim any excess fat from the chicken. Place the chicken pieces in a 6-cup (1½-qt/1.5-liter) baking dish or ovenproof casserole and brush them with the brandy, if desired. Add the garlic and half the oil to the casserole and place the chicken skin side down on top. Place in the oven for 10 minutes to brown.

✧ Turn skin side up and bake for 10 minutes longer. Season to taste with salt and pepper.

✧ Meanwhile, heat the remaining oil in a frying pan over medium heat. Add the bell peppers and cook for 2 minutes. Add the tomatoes and eggplant and cook, stirring occasionally, for 5 minutes. Pour off the oil. Pour in ½ cup (4 fl oz/125 ml) of the hot stock and add the thyme and bay leaves. Simmer for 3–4 minutes, or until the vegetables soften slightly. Remove from the heat. Spoon the vegetable mixture around the chicken in the casserole. Add the remaining hot stock and the white wine, if using. Cover and bake for about 40 minutes, or until the chicken is tender.

✧ Sprinkle the parsley over the top and serve straight from the casserole.

chicken and
brown rice *pilaf*

serves 4–6

This pilaf has a Middle
Eastern influence. Assemble it
in advance and slip it into the
oven for 30 minutes to heat
through just before serving.

3½ cups (28 fl oz/875 ml) chicken stock (broth)

1½ cups (9½ oz/300 g) long-grain brown rice

½ cup (3 oz/90 g) raisins

1 cup (8 fl oz/250 ml) freshly squeezed orange juice

3 tablespoons olive oil or vegetable oil

½ teaspoon ground ginger

½ cup (1½ oz/45 g) chopped green (spring) onions

8 chicken legs

¼ cup (1 oz/30 g) grated orange zest

½ cup (2½ oz/75 g) pine nuts

2 tablespoons finely chopped fresh mint

✤ Preheat the oven to 350°F (180°C/Gas Mark 4).

✤ Combine 3 cups (24 fl oz/750 ml) of the chicken stock with the brown rice in a 6-cup (1½-qt/1.5-liter) ovenproof casserole or baking dish. Cover and bake for 40 minutes.

✤ Meanwhile, combine the raisins and orange juice in a small bowl and set aside to soak. Heat the oil in a frying pan over medium heat, stir in the ginger and onions, and cook for 1 minute.

✤ Add the chicken legs and cook, turning as they become golden, for 3–4 minutes on each side. Remove the chicken and set aside. Pour off the oil from the pan. Add the remaining ½ cup (4 fl oz/125 ml) stock and bring to a boil. Deglaze the pan by stirring to dislodge any browned bits stuck to the bottom of the pan.

✤ Remove the casserole from the oven and stir the onion–stock mixture into the rice. Mix in the raisins, orange juice, orange zest, and pine nuts. Add the chicken, cover, and return to the oven. Bake for 30 minutes. Sprinkle with the mint and serve straight from the casserole.

mexican taco pie

PIE

Pastry for Single-crust Pie (page 291)

½ cup (2 oz/60 g) finely crushed corn chips

¼ teaspoon ground paprika (optional)

1 lb (500 g) ground (minced) beef

1 small onion, chopped

2 cloves garlic, chopped

2 teaspoons chili powder

¼ teaspoon salt

¼ teaspoon ground cumin

1 can (14 oz/440 g) undrained tomatoes, cut up

1 can (4 oz/125 g) diced green chiles, drained

½ cup (4 oz/125 g) packaged cream cheese, cubed

1 can (8 oz/250 g) red kidney beans, drained and rinsed

1 egg, beaten

GARNISH

1 cup shredded lettuce

½ cup (2 oz/60 g) shredded Cheddar cheese

1 tomato, chopped

⅓ cup (2½ fl oz/80 ml) sour cream

¼ cup (1 oz/60 g) coarsely crushed corn chips

❖ Prepare pastry as directed, stirring the crushed corn chips and paprika, if desired, into the flour and salt before mixing. Roll out and line a 9-inch (23-cm) pie plate with pastry. Trim and crimp edge of pastry.

❖ Cook the beef, onion, and garlic in a medium frying pan until the meat is brown and the onion is tender. Drain off any fat. Stir in chili powder, salt, and cumin. Add undrained tomatoes, chiles, cream cheese, and kidney beans, stirring until the cheese has melted.

❖ Preheat the oven to 375°F (190°C/Gas Mark 4). Stir about 1 cup of the meat mixture into the egg. Return all to pan and mix well. Transfer filling to pie shell. To prevent overbrowning, cover the edge of the pie with foil. Bake for 25 minutes. Remove the foil and bake for about 20 minutes more, or until heated through and the crust is golden. Let rest 10 minutes before serving.

❖ For garnish, top the pie with lettuce, cheese, tomato, sour cream, and crushed corn chips.

recipe variations

Crushed corn chips in the crust give this dinner pie extra flavor and crunch. For variety, experiment with white, yellow, and even blue corn chips in the pastry and on top.

lasagne
with four cheeses

serves 6–8

BÉCHAMEL SAUCE

3½ cups (28 fl oz/875 ml) milk

1 sprig fresh rosemary

⅓ cup (3 oz/90 g) unsalted butter

¼ cup (1½ oz/45 g) all-purpose (plain) flour

salt and ground black pepper

GARLIC BREAD CRUMBS

1 loaf good-quality country-style bread,
about 8 oz (250 g), cut into 1-inch
(2.5-cm) cubes

1 tablespoon chopped garlic, or to taste

salt and ground black pepper

extra-virgin olive oil, as needed

CHEESE MIXTURE

½ cup (2 oz/60 g) walnuts

1½ cups (12 oz/375 g) ricotta cheese

¾ cup (6 oz/185 g) mascarpone cheese

¾ cup (3 oz/90 g) shredded Fontina cheese

2 cups (8 oz/250 g) freshly grated
Parmesan cheese

1 tablespoon chopped fresh rosemary

3 tablespoons chopped fresh parsley

20 sheets "no-boil" (instant) lasagne

For the béchamel sauce, heat the milk in a saucepan with the rosemary sprig over medium–low heat until small bubbles appear along the pan edge. Meanwhile, melt the butter in a small saucepan over medium–low heat. Add the flour and whisk to form a smooth paste. Reduce the heat to low and cook, stirring, for about 2 minutes. When the milk is hot, gradually add it to the butter-flour mixture, whisking constantly. Simmer over medium heat for about 20 minutes, or until the sauce thickens enough to coat a spoon. Remove and discard the rosemary sprig. Season to taste with salt and pepper. Set aside to cool.

Preheat the oven to 350°F (180°C/Gas Mark 4). For the bread crumbs, pulse the bread cubes in a food processor fitted with a metal blade until reduced to coarse crumbs. Combine the crumbs in a large bowl with the garlic, and salt and pepper to taste. Add enough olive oil to moisten the mixture slightly. Spread the crumbs on a baking sheet and bake for 2–4 minutes, or until barely golden.

Spread the walnuts on a baking sheet and toast for about 10 minutes, or until golden and fragrant. Let cool. Increase the oven temperature to 375°F (190°C/Gas Mark 4). Combine the toasted walnuts in a large bowl with the ricotta, mascarpone, Fontina, half the Parmesan, the rosemary, parsley, and salt and pepper to taste. Mix well. Add about 1 cup (8 fl oz/250 ml) of the béchamel and stir vigorously to mix.

Bring a deep pot of lightly salted water to a rolling boil. Using tongs, dip the lasagne sheets into the boiling water for 10 seconds, then lay them on tea towels to drain.

lasagne with four cheeses

Few baked pastas are as rich and satisfying as this dish from northern Italy.

"No-boil" lasagne sheets have a marvelous tender texture but, despite the name, it is wise to dip them briefly in boiling water for the best result. Regular lasagne sheets, softened following the directions on the package, can also be used for this dish.

❖ Spread a thin layer of béchamel sauce over the bottom of a 13- x 9- x 2-inch (33- x 23- x 5-cm) lasagne pan. Top with a layer of pasta, then with a layer of the cheese mixture. Top with a layer ¼ inch (6 mm) thick of the béchamel sauce. Sprinkle with 1 tablespoon of the remaining Parmesan. Top with another layer of pasta sheets. Alternate layers of the cheese mixture and béchamel and Parmesan, until all the ingredients except the Parmesan are used up, ending with béchamel. Scatter the remaining Parmesan and the bread crumbs over the top.

❖ Cover and bake for 35–40 minutes, or until the dish is bubbling. Uncover and bake for about 10 minutes longer, or until the bread crumbs are crunchy.

❖ Let stand for 5–10 minutes before serving.

bacon and chicken
casserole

serves 4

1 medium leek, halved lengthwise

2 tablespoons olive oil,
plus 1 tablespoon extra

2 tablespoons (1 oz/30 g) butter

8 chicken drumsticks, lightly dusted with
all-purpose (plain) flour

4 slices (rashers) bacon, rind removed

4 cloves garlic, cut into slivers

2 ribs (sticks) celery, cut into small pieces

8 baby carrots, peeled

1 cup (8 fl oz/250 ml) chicken stock

½ cup (4 fl oz/125 ml) dry sherry

½ teaspoon red pepper flakes

salt and ground black pepper

½ cup (½ oz/15 g) chopped parsley

✧ Wash and drain the leek, pat dry, and chop.

✧ Heat half the oil and butter in a large frying pan and cook the chicken legs in 2 batches, using the remaining butter and oil for the second batch. Cook, turning, for 3–4 minutes, or until golden brown. Wrap each leg in a bacon slice. Place in the slow cooker.

✧ Heat the extra oil in the frying pan. Add the leek and garlic and cook, stirring, for 2–3 minutes, or until lightly browned. Stir in the celery, carrots, chicken stock, and sherry and pour over the chicken legs in the slow cooker. Sprinkle on the red pepper flakes and season to taste with salt and pepper.

✧ Put on the lid and cook casserole on Low for 7–9 hours. Sprinkle with the chopped parsley and serve with saffron-flavored rice.

serves 6–8

4 lb (2 kg) boned and rolled turkey breast

3 tablespoons butter

2 tablespoons vegetable oil

1 large sweet onion, cut into thin wedges

2 medium carrots, cut into thick batons 2 inches (5 cm) long

2 medium sweet potatoes, cut into thick batons 2 inches (5 cm) long

½ cup (4 fl oz/125 ml) white wine

1 cup (6 oz/185 g) dried apricots

½ cup (2 oz/60 g) raisins

½ cup (5 oz/150 g) apricot jam

1 cup (8 fl oz/250 ml) fresh or frozen orange juice

2 sprigs fresh oregano

salt and ground black pepper

❖ Tie the turkey breast securely at intervals with string to make an even roll, and pat dry with paper towels. Heat half the butter and oil in a large frying pan. Cook the turkey breast, turning, until golden brown all over. Transfer to the slow cooker.

❖ Heat the remaining butter and oil in the frying pan. Add the onion wedges, carrots, and sweet potatoes. Cook, stirring, for 2–3 minutes, or until softened and browned a little. Add the white wine then pour the mixture over the turkey in the slow cooker.

❖ Scatter the apricots and raisins into the Cooker. Whisk the jam in a small bowl with the orange juice until smooth. Pour over the turkey. Add the oregano sprigs and season with salt and pepper. Put on the lid and cook on Low for 10–12 hours.

❖ To serve, remove the turkey breast and place on a cutting board. Remove and discard the string used to tie the roll. Cut the meat into slices ½ inch (1 cm) thick and serve with the vegetables and cooking juices.

turkey breast stew with apricots and sweet potato

roast pork
with glazed pears

serves 6

6 lb (3 kg) pork roast

coarse salt

6 small firm pears

2 cups (16 fl oz/500 ml)
semi-sweet white wine

1 cup (8 fl oz/250 ml) water

¼ cup (2 oz/60 g)
granulated sugar

salt and ground
black pepper

all-purpose (plain)
flour, to thicken gravy

❖ Preheat the oven to 425°F (210°C/Gas Mark 5).

❖ Score the rind of the pork, wipe over, and rub
with coarse salt. Bake on a rack in a roasting pan
for 30 minutes, turning once, then reduce the heat
to 350°F (180°C/Gas Mark 4) and cook for a further
2–2¼ hours, or until the roast is done.

❖ Peel, core, and cut the pears into fourths.
Simmer in a small saucepan with the wine, water,
and sugar. When just tender, remove with a slotted
spoon and set aside. Continue to boil the cooking
liquid until well reduced and syrupy.

❖ Transfer the roast to a large platter and set aside
to rest for 15–20 minutes before carving. Pour off
the fat from the roasting pan, leaving any meat
juices. Add the reduced liquid from the pears to the
pan juices and boil to make a gravy. Thicken with a
little flour and season to taste with salt and pepper.

❖ Arrange the pear wedges around the roast
pork and serve at once. Pass the gravy separately
in a small pitcher.

stuffed
red bell peppers

serves 4

4 large red bell peppers
(capsicums)

2 tablespoons olive oil

1 medium yellow onion, diced

2 cloves garlic, finely chopped

¾ lb (375 g) lean ground
(minced) beef

2 tablespoons
ketchup (tomato sauce)

2 teaspoon
Worcestershire sauce

½ teaspoon dried oregano

½ cup (4 fl oz/125 ml)
beef stock, plus 1 cup
(8 fl oz/250 ml) extra

1 cup cooked rice,
or small macaroni, or orzo
(rice-shaped pasta)

❖ Slice the tops off the bell peppers and discard the ribs and seeds. Finely chop the bell pepper flesh from the tops.

❖ Heat the oil in a large frying pan on medium heat and cook the chopped bell pepper, onion, and garlic for 2–3 minutes, or until softened. Increase the heat to high and stir in the ground beef. Cook, stirring and breaking up any lumps with a fork, for 3–4 minutes, or until the meat is lightly browned.

❖ Remove from the heat and stir in the ketchup, Worcestershire sauce, oregano, ½ cup (4 fl oz/125 ml) beef stock, and the cooked rice.

❖ Fill the bell peppers with the mixture and stand them, spaced so they are not touching, in the slow cooker. Pour on the extra beef stock. Put on the lid and cook on Low for 6–8 hours. Serve hot.

turkey enchilada stack

serves 4

five 6-inch (15-cm) corn tortillas

*1 jar (12 oz/375 g) salsa
(hot or mild)*

*1 can (14 oz/440 g)
kidney beans*

*1 cup (6½ oz/200 g) fresh
or frozen corn kernels*

*½ red bell pepper (capsicum),
seeded and thinly sliced*

*1 cup (6 oz/175 g) shredded
cooked turkey*

*1 cup (4 oz/125 g)
shredded Cheddar or
Monterey Jack cheese*

*¼ cup (½ oz/15 g) chopped
fresh cilantro (coriander)*

❖ Make foil handles to aid removal of the tortillas after cooking. Make three 18- x 2-inch (45- x 5-cm) strips of heavy-duty foil or regular foil folded double. Crisscross the foil strips in a spoke design over the base and up the sides of the slow cooker.

❖ Place 1 tortilla over the base of the slow cooker. Spread with one fourth each of the salsa, beans, corn, bell pepper, turkey, and cheese (reserve a little cheese to sprinkle over the top of the stack of tortillas).

❖ Repeat the layers, finishing with a tortilla and the reserved cheese. Put on the lid and cook on Low for 6–8 hours, or High for 3–4 hours. Pull out with the aid of the foil strips and sprinkle with the chopped cilantro. Cut into fourths and serve hot.

moussaka

serves 8–10

3 lb (1.5 kg) eggplant (aubergine)

salt

olive oil, for brushing

MEAT SAUCE

2 tablespoons olive oil

3 large yellow onions, chopped

2 lb (1 kg) ground (minced) lean lamb

3 cups (18 oz/560 g) canned chopped
plum (Roma) tomatoes

3 tablespoons tomato paste

4 cloves garlic, finely chopped

1/2 cup (4 fl oz/125 ml) red wine

1 tablespoon dried oregano

3/4 cup (1 oz/30 g) chopped fresh
flat-leaf (Italian) parsley

1 tablespoon ground cinnamon

pinch of ground cloves or allspice

salt and ground black pepper

BÉCHAMEL SAUCE

3 tablespoons (1½ oz/50 g)
unsalted butter

3 tablespoons all-purpose (plain) flour

3 cups (24 fl oz/750 ml) hot milk

1/2 teaspoon grated nutmeg

salt and ground white pepper

3 eggs, lightly beaten

1 cup (8 oz/250 g) whole-milk
ricotta cheese

TO ASSEMBLE

1/2 cup (2 oz/60 g) fine dried
bread crumbs

1 cup (4 oz/125 g) grated kefalotiri
or Parmesan cheese

moussaka

❖ Peel the eggplant, if desired, and cut into slices ½ inch (1 cm) thick. Place the slices in a colander, sprinkle with salt, and let stand for 1 hour to draw off the bitter juices.

❖ Meanwhile, make the meat sauce. Heat the olive oil in a large frying pan over medium heat and cook the onions for about 8 minutes, or until tender. Add the lamb and cook for 5–7 minutes, or until the meat loses its redness and starts to brown. Add the tomatoes, tomato paste, garlic, wine, oregano, parsley, cinnamon, and ground cloves, and simmer over low heat for about 45 minutes, or until thickened and most of the liquid is absorbed. If it begins to look too dry, add a little water. Adjust the seasoning to taste with salt, pepper, and the spices. Set aside.

❖ Preheat the oven to 400°F (200°C/Gas Mark 5). Rinse the eggplant slices with cool water, drain well, and pat dry with paper towels. Place on baking sheets, brush the tops with olive oil, and bake, turning once and brushing on the second side with oil, for 15–20 minutes, or until tender and golden. Drain on paper towels.

❖ For the béchamel sauce, melt the butter over low heat in a small saucepan. Whisk in the flour and increase the heat to medium. Cook, stirring, for 2 minutes (do not allow to brown). Gradually whisk in the hot milk and bring to the boil. Reduce the heat to low and simmer for 2–3 minutes, or until thickened. Add the nutmeg, season to taste with salt and pepper, and remove from the heat. Whisk the eggs and ricotta together in a small bowl until well blended, then whisk into the hot sauce.

moussaka

❖ Reduce the oven temperature to 350°F (180°C/Gas Mark 4).

❖ To assemble the moussaka, oil an 11- x 15-inch (28- x 37.5-cm) baking pan. Sprinkle half the bread crumbs on the bottom of the pan. Arrange half of the eggplant slices in the pan and spoon the meat sauce over them. Layer the remaining eggplant slices on top and pour the béchamel evenly over the surface. Sprinkle with the remaining bread crumbs and then with the cheese.

❖ Bake the moussaka for about 45 minutes, or until it is heated through and the top is golden brown. Remove from the oven and let rest for 15 minutes before cutting into squares to serve.

recipe variations

For a vegetarian version of moussaka that will serve 5–6 people, simply omit the ground lamb from the sauce recipe and reduce the cooking time for the sauce to 20 minutes. Complete the dish in the same way as given for the meat version.

chicken
with fennel and lemon

4 medium boneless, skinless chicken breast halves, about 2 lb (1 kg) total weight

2 tablespoons butter

1 tablespoon vegetable oil

1 medium fennel bulb, trimmed and cut into 8 wedges

1 large red (Spanish) onion, cut into 8 wedges

½ cup (4 fl oz/125 ml) white wine

¾ cup (6 fl oz/185 ml) chicken stock

1 sprig fresh thyme

4 whole cloves garlic, unpeeled

1 lemon, thinly sliced

12 green olives, pitted

fresh thyme leaves, to garnish

❖ Pat the chicken breasts dry with paper towels. Heat half the butter and all the oil in a large frying pan and brown the chicken breasts on both sides over high heat until golden. Transfer to the slow cooker.

❖ Heat the remaining butter in the frying pan and cook the fennel and onion wedges, stirring, for 2–3 minutes to soften and brown a little. Deglaze the pan with the wine and stir in the stock and thyme sprig. Pour over the chicken breasts.

❖ Add the garlic cloves and lemon to the chicken. Put on the lid and cook on Low for 6–8 hours. Add the green olives and remove the thyme sprig.

❖ To serve, squeeze the garlic out of the skin, mash with a fork, and stir through the juices. Sprinkle the chicken with fresh thyme leaves. Serve with polenta.

braised
veal shanks
with lemon, garlic, and parsley

serves 4

½ cup (2½ oz/75 g) unbleached all-purpose (plain) flour

4 veal shanks, about 4 lb (2 kg) total weight, each about 2 inches (5 cm) thick

2 tablespoons unsalted butter

2 tablespoons extra-virgin olive oil

½ cup (2½ oz/75 g) chopped yellow onion

½ cup (2½ oz/75 g) peeled, diced carrot

½ cup (2½ oz/75 g) diced celery

⅓ cup (2 oz/60 g) diced fennel bulb

1 teaspoon chopped garlic

2 teaspoons fresh marjoram leaves

2 teaspoons fresh thyme leaves

1 bay leaf

1¼ cups (8 oz/250 g) peeled, seeded, and chopped tomatoes

1 cup (8 fl oz/250 ml) dry Italian white wine

2–3 cups (16–24 fl oz/500–750 ml) meat stock, or as needed

salt and ground black pepper

steamed rice or risotto flavored with saffron, to serve

GREMOLATA

½ cup (½ oz/15 g) chopped fresh Italian (flat-leaf) parsley

1½ teaspoons chopped lemon zest

½ teaspoon chopped garlic

❖ To prepare the veal shanks, spread the flour on a plate and coat the veal shanks evenly with flour, shaking off any excess.

❖ Melt the butter with the olive oil in a large frying pan or pot over medium–high heat and brown the veal shanks for about 4 minutes per side, or until lightly browned all over. Remove the veal shanks from the pan and set aside.

❖ Reduce the heat to medium–low and cook the onion, carrot, celery, and fennel for 3–4 minutes, or until the edges of the onion are translucent—do not allow to brown. Add the garlic, marjoram, thyme, and bay leaf and stir until blended. Add the tomatoes and bring to the boil. Return the veal to the pan and cook for 1 minute. Increase the heat to high, pour in the wine, and deglaze the pan by stirring to dislodge any browned bits from the bottom of the pan.

❖ When the mixture boils, add about 2 cups (16 fl oz/500 ml) of the stock; the liquid should reach three-fourths of the way up the sides of the veal shanks. Reduce the heat to medium–low, partly cover, and simmer, turning the shanks over occasionally. Continue cooking, adding more stock as needed to keep the mixture moist, for about 2½ hours, or until the veal is tender when pierced with a fork and there are about 2 cups (16 fl oz/500 ml) of liquid and vegetables remaining. If there is too much liquid, uncover and simmer to concentrate the broth. Season to taste with salt and pepper.

braised veal shanks with lemon, garlic, and parsley

❖ While the stew is cooking, prepare the steamed rice or risotto. Just before serving, make the gremolata by tossing the parsley, lemon zest, and garlic together in a small bowl until evenly mixed.

❖ To serve, discard the bay leaf. Place a mound of rice or risotto on each individual plate. Place 1 veal shank on top of each mound of rice or risotto and spoon the broth and vegetables on top. Sprinkle with the gremolata and serve immediately.

recipe variations

Lamb shanks are also delicious prepared in this way. Allow 2 lamb shanks per person and reduce the cooking time to 2 hours. Serve with Mashed Potatoes (page 66) and ratatouille.

roman roast lamb
with rosemary and garlic

serves 4

The appearance of roast lamb on trattoria menus, especially around Rome, traditionally signals the coming of spring. Cooking lamb in this manner yields especially succulent results.

To make carving easier, ask your butcher to crack the bones between the ribs.

2 racks of lamb, 8 chops per rack, about 4 lb (2 kg) total weight, breastbone cracked between each rib

¼ cup (2 fl oz/60 ml) sunflower or canola oil

small sprigs fresh rosemary

garlic cloves, cut in fourths lengthwise

2 cups (16 fl oz/500 ml) full-bodied Italian white wine, or as needed

salt and ground black pepper

lemon wedges, to serve

◈ Using a sharp knife, score the fat on the top surface of the lamb to prevent curling and shrinking. Heat the oil in a large frying pan over high heat and brown each lamb rack for about 5 minutes, or until browned on all sides. Place the racks, bone side down, in a large roasting pan.

◈ Preheat the oven to 450°F (220°C/Gas Mark 6). Place the rosemary and garlic pieces between the chops, pushing them to the bottom where the bones are cracked and using whatever amount suits your taste. Stud the scored surface with rosemary and garlic as well. Pour white wine over the chops and into the pan to a depth of ¼ inch (6 mm) and grind pepper over the racks.

◈ Place in the center of the oven, immediately reduce the heat to 400°F (200°C/Gas Mark 5), and roast, basting once with wine, for about 1 hour, or until golden brown.

◈ Remove the pan from the oven, baste the lamb again with the wine, and cover with aluminum foil. Return to the oven and continue to roast for 20 minutes. Remove the foil, baste again, and continue to roast the lamb, uncovered, for about 10 minutes longer, or until the surface is deep brown and crisp.

◈ Let the lamb rest for 15 minutes before transferring to a cutting board and carving. If the lamb becomes cool, warm in a 225°F (105°C/Gas Mark 1) oven for 2–3 minutes just before carving. Carve into chops and distribute among warmed individual plates. Season to taste with salt and pepper and serve with lemon wedges.

duck terrine
with hazelnuts

serves 6

3 tablespoons milk

3 tablespoons Cognac

1 teaspoon (5 g) powdered unflavored
gelatin (or 2 leaves)

3½ oz (100 g) shelled hazelnuts

¾ cup (2 oz/60 g) fresh bread crumbs

1 boned duck breast
(about 8 oz/250 g), skinned

salt

1 teaspoon finely ground pepper

6½ oz (200 g) boned chicken breast meat

3½ oz (100 g) cooked ham

½ teaspoon ground allspice

1 clove garlic, crushed

1 golden (French) shallot, peeled
and crushed

1 egg

1 tablespoon peanut oil

✤ Preheat the oven to 350°F (180°C/Gas Mark 4).

✤ Combine the milk and Cognac in a small non-aluminum saucepan and sprinkle the gelatin over. Set aside to soften.

✤ Toast the hazelnuts in a small nonstick pan; set aside to cool. Remove some of the skins by rubbing the toasted nuts with a tea towel.

✤ Warm the milk, Cognac, and gelatin mixture over low heat and stir until the gelatin dissolves. Stir in the bread crumbs for 2 minutes over low heat, to make a smooth paste. Remove from the heat.

✤ Cut the duck breast into ½-inch (1-cm) slices. Season with salt and pepper. Set aside.

✤ Cut the chicken breast and ham into cubes and put them into the food processor. Add the bread paste, salt to taste, allspice, and additional pepper to taste. Process on high speed for 30 seconds. Add the garlic, shallot, and egg to the processor and mix again for 30 seconds. Transfer the mixture to a large bowl and stir in the hazelnuts.

✤ Oil a 2½-cup (20-fl oz/625-ml) ceramic terrine and coat it with a thin layer of the processed mixture. Cover with slices of duck. Continue layering in this manner, finishing with a layer of the hazelnut mixture. Press down well. Brush the surface with oil and cover the terrine tightly with foil or a lid. Bake in the preheated oven for 1¾ hours.

✤ Let the terrine cool before refrigerating for at least 12 hours before serving. Slice and serve at room temperature, with gherkins, onions, and cherries in vinegar, toast, and a green salad.

beef casserole
with onions

serves 4

With this simple and
reliable method of cooking,
you will produce a
flavorsome beef dish
that literally melts in
the mouth every time
you cook it.

2 lb (1 kg) top rump roast of beef, tied with string

salt and ground black pepper

7 whole cloves

2 lb (1 kg) large onions, cut into ½-inch (1-cm) slices

10 oz (315 g) medium spaghetti

½ cup (2 oz/60 g) finely grated Parmesan cheese

❖ Preheat the oven to 250°F (120°C/Gas Mark 1).

❖ Season the meat with salt and pepper, and stick the cloves into the roast. Line the bottom of a 16-cup (4-qt/4-l) stoneware or cast-iron pot with the onions and place the meat on top. Cover the pot, place in the oven, and cook for 5 hours, turning the meat once or twice.

❖ After 5 hours, remove the pot and lift the lid: a delicious aroma will rise from the pot where everything is golden—the inside of the pot, the meat, and the onions.

❖ Remove the string from the meat. Set the meat on a serving plate and decorate it with half of the onion rings. Cover the dish with foil or keep it warm in the turned-off oven.

❖ Bring a pot of salted water to the boil and cook the spaghetti until al dente.

❖ Pass the remaining onions and cooking juices through the medium disk of a food mill over a large pan.

❖ Drain the spaghetti. Toss with the puréed onions in the pan and reheat for 1 minute over low heat. Pour the spaghetti into a deep serving dish.

❖ Serve the beef and spaghetti at the same time. Sprinkle the spaghetti with Parmesan and pepper just before presenting the diners with the meat, which will be so tender that you can almost serve it with a spoon.

chicken with sweet potatoes

serves 6

½ cup (2½ oz/75 g) all-purpose (plain) flour, plus 2 tablespoons extra

½ teaspoon each of ground cinnamon, ground nutmeg, and onion powder

salt and ground black pepper

6 large chicken thighs, on the bone

2 sweet potatoes, peeled and cut into ½-inch (1-cm) slices

3 oz (90 g) fresh mushrooms, sliced

1 can (11 oz/345 g) condensed cream of chicken soup

½ cup (4 fl oz/125 ml) pineapple juice

1 teaspoon brown sugar

cooked rice, to serve

finely grated zest of ½ lemon

½ cup (½ oz/15 g) finely chopped parsley

❖ Combine the ½ cup flour, spices, and salt and pepper to taste in a large plastic bag. Add the chicken thighs and shake to coat them thoroughly with the mixture.

❖ Arrange the sweet potato slices on the base of the slow cooker. Place the floured chicken thighs evenly over the top. Scatter the sliced mushrooms over.

❖ Combine the extra flour in a small bowl with the soup, juice, and brown sugar. Pour the mixture on the chicken thighs, put on the lid, and cook on Low for 8–10 hours, or on High for 3–4 hours.

❖ Serve on a bed of rice, sprinkled with the combined lemon rind and parsley.

duck leg confit with warm green lentil salad

serves 4

DUCK LEG CONFIT

1 tablespoon salt

1 teaspoon cracked pepper

4 duck legs, about ¾ lb (375 g) each

4 cloves garlic, crushed

4 sprigs fresh thyme

2 bay leaves, torn in half

5 lb (2.5 kg) duck or pork fat,
cut into pieces

GREEN LENTIL SALAD

1½ cups (10 oz/315 g) dried green lentils

6 cups (48 fl oz/1.5 l) water

bouquet garni (see Glossary, page 310)

1 teaspoon salt

½ teaspoon ground black pepper

1 cup (8 fl oz/250 ml) veal or chicken stock

Vinaigrette (page 217)

2 tablespoons chopped fresh parsley

duck leg confit with warm green lentil salad

❖ To make the confit, rub the 1 tablespoon salt and the cracked pepper evenly over the duck legs and place in a shallow glass dish. Place 1 clove garlic, a thyme sprig, and half a bay leaf on each leg. Cover with plastic wrap and refrigerate overnight.

❖ Next day, render the duck or pork fat by placing the fat in a heavy-bottomed pan over very low heat. Cook slowly for 2–3 hours, or until all the fat liquefies, any tissue has become crisp, and the impurities sink to the bottom of the pan. Pour the clear fat through a fine-mesh sieve lined with cheesecloth (muslin) into a large saucepan.

❖ Cut the duck legs in half to separate the thighs and drumsticks. Place the meat, along with the garlic, thyme, and bay leaves, in the melted fat. Bring to the boil, then reduce the heat to medium–low and simmer, uncovered, for about 2½ hours, or until the meat is easily pierced with a fork and the juices run clear.

❖ Using tongs, carefully transfer the meat to a deep earthenware bowl or terrine. Line a fine-mesh sieve with cheesecloth (muslin) and drain enough of the fat through the sieve to cover the meat completely. Let cool until the fat hardens fully. Make sure that the duck pieces are totally sealed in the fat so that no air can reach them. Cover and refrigerate for at least 24 hours, or for up to 3 weeks.

❖ When ready to make the lentil salad, preheat the oven to 450°F (220°C/Gas Mark 6).

duck leg confit with warm green lentil salad

To make the lentil salad, rinse the lentils under cold running water. Bring the water to the boil in a large saucepan. Add the lentils, bouquet garni, the 1 teaspoon salt, and the pepper to the boiling water. Reduce the heat to medium, cover, and simmer for 20–25 minutes, or until the lentils are tender.

Meanwhile, remove the duck legs from the fat, scraping off as much of the fat as possible. Place the legs, skin side down, in a roasting pan. Place in the oven for about 15 minutes, or until the skin is crispy and the meat is heated through.

When the lentils are cooked, drain them in a fine-mesh sieve. Discard the bouquet garni and place the lentils in a saucepan. Add the stock and vinaigrette and bring to the boil. Stir in the parsley, then taste and adjust the seasoning, if necessary.

Spoon a bed of lentils onto warmed individual plates and place the hot duck legs on top. Serve immediately.

vinaigrette

2 tablespoons sherry vinegar

2 tablespoons balsamic vinegar

1 teaspoon salt

¼ teaspoon ground white pepper

⅔ cup (5 oz/150 ml) olive oil

Using a wire whisk, whisk the vinegars, salt, and pepper together in a small bowl.

Whisking continuously, add the olive oil in a slow, steady stream, whisking for about 1 minute, or until well blended and emulsified.

makes about 1 cup (8 fl oz/250 ml)

slow-cooked
vegetables *and* grains

candied leeks

serves 3

2 tablespoons butter

2 teaspoons superfine (caster) sugar

salt

13 oz (410 g) lower white parts of leeks, blanched

✧ Preheat the oven to 400°F (200°C/Gas Mark 5).

✧ Combine the butter, sugar, salt, and 2 tablespoons of water in a 9-inch (23-cm) baking dish. Place the dish in the oven and let the butter melt.

✧ Add the leeks, turning them to coat with the butter-sugar mixture.

✧ Cover the dish with foil. Cook for 40–45 minutes, or until no water remains and leeks are caramelized.

✧ Serve in the baking dish, hot from the oven.

green chile and
black bean bake

serves 4–6

1 tablespoon vegetable oil

1 large yellow onion, chopped

1 green bell pepper (capsicum), seeded and chopped

2 cloves garlic, chopped

1 jalapeño chile, seeded and diced

2 teaspoons chili powder

1 teaspoon ground cumin

½ teaspoon dried oregano leaves

3 cans (each 14 oz/440 g) black beans, drained

3 ripe tomatoes, seeded and chopped

1 cup (8 fl oz/250 ml) flat beer

1 cup (8 fl oz/250 ml) ketchup (tomato sauce)

salt and ground black pepper

tortillas, sour cream, and shredded Cheddar cheese, to serve

❖ Heat oil in a large frying pan and cook the onion, bell pepper, garlic, and chile for 3–4 minutes. Stir in the chili powder, cumin, and oregano leaves and cook for 1 minute.

❖ Stir in beans, tomatoes, beer, and ketchup. Season to taste with salt and pepper.

❖ Pour into the slow cooker. Put on the lid and cook on Low for 4–6 hours. Serve with tortillas and top with sour cream and shredded cheese.

two-potato bake

serves 4–6

1 lb (500 g) potatoes

1 lb (500 g) sweet potatoes (kumera)

1 large yellow onion, sliced thinly into rings

1/2 cup (1/2 oz/15 g) chopped fresh parsley, plus extra to garnish

1 teaspoon caraway seeds

salt and ground black pepper

spray cooking oil

1 1/2 cups (12 fl oz/375 ml) chicken stock

1 tablespoon butter, chopped

❖ Peel and cut the potatoes and sweet potatoes into slices 1/2 inch (1 cm) thick.

❖ Arrange a layer of the potatoes and sweet potatoes in the slow cooker. Scatter with the onion slices, parsley, and caraway seeds, and season well with salt and pepper. Repeat the layers, spraying each lightly with spray cooking oil, until the vegetables are all used.

❖ Pour in the stock and dot the top with pieces of butter. Put on the lid and cook on Low for 7–9 hours, or until the potatoes are tender. Sprinkle with the extra parsley and serve hot.

rainbow lasagne

serves 6–8

5 tablespoons (2½ oz/75 g) butter

¼ cup (1½ oz/45 g) all-purpose (plain) flour

4 cups (1 qt/1 liter) milk

½ teaspoon sharp mustard

salt and ground white pepper

2 cups (8 oz/250 g) shredded mozzarella cheese

1 lb (500 g) chopped frozen or fresh spinach

½ teaspoon grated nutmeg

2 medium onions, sliced

3 tablespoons olive oil

1 large red bell pepper (capsicum), sliced

2 cups (12 oz/375 g) corn kernels

1 lb (500 g) curly instant lasagne or partly cooked dried lasagne

3 large tomatoes, sliced

1½ cups (12 fl oz/375 ml) Tomato Sauce (page 247)

❖ Melt the butter in a medium saucepan and stir in the flour. Remove from the heat, add the milk, and stir until smooth. Return to moderate heat and stir until thickened, adding the mustard and salt and pepper to taste. Stir in three-fourths of the cheese, cover the top with a piece of plastic wrap to prevent a skin forming, and set aside.

❖ Cook the spinach in a tightly covered pan over low heat, removing the lid and increasing the heat after a short while to boil off the liquid. Season to taste with salt and pepper and add the nutmeg. Cook the onions in 2 tablespoons of the oil until softened and lightly colored. Cook the bell pepper separately in the remaining oil. Mix half the onion with the spinach and one-third of the cheese sauce. Cook the corn in lightly salted water, drain, and mix with the remaining onion and one-third of the cheese sauce.

❖ Preheat the oven to 350°F (180°C/Gas Mark 4).

❖ Grease a large lasagne dish and cover the bottom with lasagne sheets. Layer the ingredients in the lasagne dish in the following sequence: the spinach mixture, another layer of lasagne sheets, the cooked bell peppers and sliced tomatoes, the tomato sauce, another layer of lasagne sheets, the corn sauce, the remaining cheese sauce, and the remaining shredded cheese. Bake for about 45 minutes.

❖ The lasagne can be prepared up to 24 hours in advance and refrigerated until ready to cook. Assembled uncooked lasagne can be frozen. To cook frozen lasagne, preheat the oven to 350°F (180°C/Gas Mark 4) and cook for about 1 hour.

mushrooms
with tomatoes

½ oz (15 g) dried porcini mushrooms

1 lb (500 g) whole button mushrooms

2 tablespoons olive oil

1 red (Spanish) onion, finely chopped

2 cloves garlic, finely chopped

1 can (14 oz/440 g) chopped tomatoes

1 teaspoon sugar

salt and ground black pepper

½ cup (½ oz/15 g) chopped parsley

◈ Soak the porcini mushrooms in ½ cup (4 fl oz/ 125 ml) hot water for 5 minutes. Chop the porcini mushrooms finely and reserve the soaking liquid. Wipe the button mushrooms clean with damp paper towels.

◈ Heat the oil in a large frying pan and cook the onion and garlic for 2–3 minutes. Add the porcini mushrooms and their liquid and stir over medium–high heat until the liquid has evaporated.

◈ Stir in the button mushrooms, tomatoes, and sugar, and season to taste with salt and pepper. Transfer to the slow cooker. Put on the lid and cook on Low for 2–3 hours. Just before serving, stir in the parsley. Serve hot with warm crusty bread.

potato casserole

serves 4

olive oil, for deep-frying

4 large potatoes
(about 1½ lb/750 g), peeled
and cut into ½-inch
(1-cm) slices

2 eggs, beaten

all-purpose (plain) flour,
for coating

4 cloves garlic, finely chopped

2 small onions, finely chopped

4 small tomatoes, peeled and
finely chopped

1 teaspoon sugar

1⅔ cups (13 fl oz/410 ml)
beef stock

salt

❖ Heat the oil in a medium frying pan. Dip the potato slices into the beaten egg and then into the flour. Fry until golden on both sides. Transfer to a heatproof casserole, leaving a little oil in the pan. Fry the garlic and onion, add the chopped tomato, and cook over low heat until it has been reduced a little.

❖ Add the sugar and ½ tablespoon of flour, stir well, and pour over the potatoes. Add the stock and a little salt, to taste. Cover and cook over low heat for 30–45 minutes, or until the potatoes are tender when pierced with the point of a sharp knife. Serve hot.

baked eggplant, tomato, and pasta gratin

serves 6

3 medium eggplant (aubergines)
(about 3 lb/1.5 kg total weight)

salt

TOMATO SAUCE

2 tablespoons olive oil

2 onions, chopped

2 cloves garlic, chopped

1 can (14 oz/440 g) plum
tomatoes, undrained

2 tablespoons tomato paste

2 teaspoons dried basil

1 teaspoon dried oregano

ground black pepper

extra olive oil, for frying eggplant

8 oz (250 g) dried penne or other
short pasta

about 10 oz (300 g) mozzarella
cheese, sliced

✧ Wash the eggplant and cut crosswise into thin slices. Arrange the slices in a colander and sprinkle the cut surfaces with salt. Stand for about 30 minutes to degorge the bitter juices. Rinse the eggplant slices under cold running water and pat the slices thoroughly dry with paper towels.

✧ For the tomato sauce, heat the olive oil in a large saucepan. Add the onion and garlic and cook until the onion is softened. Add the undrained tomatoes, tomato paste, basil, and oregano, and bring the sauce to the boil. Simmer for about 30 minutes, or until well thickened. Season to taste with salt and pepper.

✧ Heat 2–3 tablespoons of olive oil in a large frying pan. Working in batches, fry the eggplant slices on both sides, until cooked through and lightly golden. Add more oil as necessary. Drain the eggplant slices on paper towels.

✧ Preheat the oven to 350°F (180°C/Gas Mark 4). Grease a large gratin dish (about 8-cup/2-qt/2-l capacity).

✧ Cook the pasta in boiling salted water until al dente. Drain and stir into the tomato sauce. Layer the ingredients in the gratin dish in the following sequence: one-third of the eggplant slices, half the tomato pasta sauce, one-third of the eggplant slices, half the mozzarella slices, half the tomato pasta sauce, one-third of the eggplant slices, half the mozzarella slices.

✧ Bake, uncovered, for 30 minutes, or until the cheese on top is melted and golden. Serve hot.

sweet-and-sour
red cabbage

serves 4

½ red cabbage
(about 1 lb/500 g)

2 tablespoons butter

1 yellow onion, roughly chopped

1 teaspoon caraway seeds

1 large green apple,
cored and roughly chopped

⅓ cup (2¾ fl oz/80 ml)
red wine vinegar

⅓ cup (2¾ fl oz/80 ml) chicken stock

2 tablespoons redcurrant jelly

salt and ground black pepper

❖ Discard the tough outer layers and cut the cabbage into fourths, removing the center core. Roughly chop the cabbage into small pieces.

❖ Heat the butter in a large frying pan and cook the onion and caraway seeds for 2–3 minutes. Transfer to the slow cooker.

❖ Stir in the cabbage, chopped apple, red wine vinegar, and stock. Put on the lid and cook on Low for 4–6 hours. Stir in the redcurrant jelly and season to taste with salt and pepper.

❖ Serve the sweet-and-sour cabbage with pork or sausage dishes.

caponata

serves 4–6

3 tablespoons olive oil

1 sweet onion, cut into thin wedges

3 cloves garlic, peeled and sliced thinly

1 rib (stick) celery, cut into 1-inch (2.5-cm) slices

2 red bell peppers (capsicums), seeded and cut into 1-inch (2.5-cm) pieces

1 medium eggplant (aubergine), cut into 1-inch (2.5-cm) cubes

1 can (14 oz/440 g) chopped tomatoes

1 tablespoon tomato paste

2 tablespoons red wine vinegar

1 tablespoon brown sugar

salt and ground black pepper

10 black olives, pitted and chopped

2 tablespoons capers

⬥ Heat the oil in a large frying pan and cook the onion, garlic, and celery for 2–3 minutes. Add the red bell pepper and eggplant, stir, and cook on medium–high heat for 4–5 minutes, or until the eggplant is lightly browned.

⬥ Transfer to the slow cooker. Stir in the chopped tomatoes, tomato paste, vinegar, and sugar. Season to taste with salt and pepper.

⬥ Put on the lid and cook on Low for 6–8 hours. The vegetables should be soft, but not mushy. Stir in the olives and capers. Serve warm or at room temperature.

collard greens
with bacon

serves 4

A time-honored tradition in southern kitchens in the United States, collard greens are typically cooked for a long time to temper their tough texture and smooth out their bitter flavor. If you cook them a day ahead and then reheat them, they will taste even better. These greens are the perfect foil for rich main dishes.

2 teaspoons olive oil

6 thick-cut slices (rashers) bacon, chopped

2 large cloves garlic, chopped

1/8 teaspoon salt

1/4 teaspoon ground black pepper

1/8 teaspoon cayenne pepper

2 tablespoons cider vinegar mixed with 2 cups (16 fl oz/500 ml) water

5 bunches collard greens, about 5 lb (2.5 kg) total weight, stemmed and carefully washed

Tabasco or other hot-pepper sauce (optional)

❖ Heat the olive oil in a large stockpot over medium heat. Add the bacon and fry, stirring constantly, for 3–4 minutes, or until cooked through but not crisp. Remove the pot from the heat and, using a slotted spoon, transfer the bacon to a dish. Set aside. Pour off all but 2 tablespoons of the bacon drippings from the pot.

❖ Return the stockpot to medium heat. Add the garlic, salt, and black and cayenne peppers and cook for 1 minute. Carefully pour in the vinegar-water mixture, stirring until blended. Return the bacon to the pot and boil for 1–2 minutes.

❖ Reduce the heat to medium–low and add the greens. (Do not worry if the pan is very full; the greens will cook down quickly.) Cover and simmer for 10 minutes, then remove the lid and stir well. Add a few drops of Tabasco, if desired, cover again, and reduce the heat to very low.

❖ Simmer, stirring occasionally and adding a little water, if necessary, to keep the greens damp, for about 1½ hours, or until the greens are tender.

❖ Spoon the greens into a warmed serving dish and serve immediately.

baked beans

serves 6

Dried beans kept the early American settlers going through many a long, cold winter. Nonperishable, rich in protein, and flavorsome, baked beans have been a necessity and a favorite for generations. The flavor of these beans is even better if they are reheated the day after they are cooked.

Serve with hamburgers or broiled (grilled) hot dogs.

2½ cups (1 lb/500 g) dried small white (navy) or Great Northern beans

1 yellow onion, coarsely chopped

¼ cup (3 oz/90 g) dark molasses (treacle)

2 tablespoons firmly packed light brown sugar

1 tablespoon dry mustard

1 tablespoon Worcestershire sauce

½ cup (4 fl oz/125 ml) apple cider

2 tablespoons bourbon whisky

¼ cup (2 fl oz/60 ml) tomato pasta sauce, purchased or homemade

½ teaspoon salt

¼ teaspoon ground pepper

1 cup (8 fl oz/250 ml) water

8 oz (250 g) cooked ham, preferably honey-baked, cut into ¼-inch (6-mm) cubes

❖ Pick over the beans, discarding any grit, and rinse with water. Place in a bowl, add water to cover by 2 inches (5 cm), and soak overnight. Drain.

❖ Bring a large saucepan three-fourths full of water to the boil. Add the drained beans and the onion and return to the boil. Reduce the heat to medium–low, partly cover, and simmer for 1–1½ hours, or until the beans are very tender. Drain well and set aside.

❖ Preheat the oven to 350°F (180°C/Gas Mark 4).

❖ Combine the molasses in a saucepan over medium heat with the brown sugar, mustard, Worcestershire sauce, apple cider, whisky, tomato pasta sauce, salt, pepper, and water. Bring to simmering point, stirring until the sugar dissolves. Continue cooking for 1–2 minutes to blend the flavors.

❖ Combine the beans and sauce in a 1½-qt (1.5-l) baking dish and mix well. Add a little more water if the mixture looks dry. Stir in the ham. Cover and bake for 35 minutes. Uncover and increase the heat to 400°F (200°C/Gas Mark 5). Continue to bake for 45–60 minutes, or until the liquid is almost gone.

❖ Serve immediately, or let cool, cover, and refrigerate overnight. To serve, let the chilled beans return to room temperature, then place in a 375°F (190°C/Gas Mark 4) oven for about 25 minutes, or until heated through.

mediterranean stuffed eggplant

serves 4

The eggplant halves can be prepared ahead of time and served with a green salad and crusty bread for a special luncheon. If you are feeding vegetarians, simply omit the meat.

2 globe eggplants (aubergines), about 1 lb (500 g) each

salt

¼ cup (2 fl oz/60 ml) olive oil

6 oz (185 g) ground (minced) ham or veal (optional)

2 medium onions, peeled and chopped

2 cloves garlic, cut in half

4 ripe tomatoes, thinly sliced

2 cups (16 fl oz/500 ml) vegetable stock

1 cup (6 oz/185 g) Arborio or other short-grain rice

1 teaspoon dried marjoram

1 teaspoon dried thyme

salt and ground pepper

2 tablespoons chopped fresh parsley

❖ Preheat the oven to 350°F (180°C/Gas Mark 4). Cut the eggplant in half lengthwise, and sprinkle the cut sides with salt. Place cut side down in a colander to drain for 30 minutes. Heat half the oil in a large frying pan over medium heat. Add the ham or veal, if using, and cook for 3–4 minutes. Add the onion and garlic and cook for 2–3 minutes, or until soft. Stir in half of the sliced tomatoes and ½ cup (4 fl oz/125 ml) of the stock. Cover and simmer over low heat for 5 minutes.

❖ Meanwhile, rinse the eggplant halves under cold water. Scoop out most of the flesh, leaving shells about 1 inch (2.5 cm) thick. Coarsely chop the flesh and stir into the tomato mixture. Add the rice, marjoram, thyme, and 1 cup (8 fl oz/250 ml) of stock, stirring to mix well. Cover and simmer over medium heat for 15 minutes, stirring a few times to prevent sticking. Discard the garlic halves and season to taste with salt and pepper.

❖ Fill each eggplant shell with one-fourth of the stuffing. Place in a baking dish and pour the remaining oil around the eggplant. Place the remaining sliced tomato around the eggplant and pour in the remaining ½ cup (4 fl oz/125 ml) stock. Bake for 40–45 minutes, or until the eggplant halves are tender.

❖ During the baking time, stir and mash the tomatoes with a spoon and baste the eggplant with the tomato-stock mixture several times.

❖ Place the eggplant halves on a platter, sprinkle with parsley, and serve hot with the sauce from the dish spooned over the top. (This dish is also delicious served at room temperature.)

3 tablespoons olive oil

1 medium sweet onion, cut into thin wedges

3 cloves garlic, finely chopped

1 lb (500 g) globe eggplant (aubergine), cut into chunks

2 medium zucchini (courgettes), cut into slices 1 inch (2.5 cm) thick

1 rib (stick) celery, cut into slices 1 inch (2.5 cm) thick

1 red bell pepper (capsicum), seeded and cut into 1-inch (2.5-cm) chunks

1 lb (500 g) ripe tomatoes, peeled, seeded, and chopped

1 tablespoon tomato paste

1 teaspoon sugar

2 sprigs fresh thyme

salt and ground black pepper

extra fresh thyme leaves, for sprinkling

2 tablespoons capers

❖ Heat the oil in a large frying pan over medium heat and cook the onion and garlic for 2–3 minutes. Add the eggplant and cook, stirring, over medium–high heat for 4–5 minutes, or until the eggplant is lightly browned.

❖ Transfer to the slow cooker. Stir in the zucchini, celery, bell pepper, chopped tomatoes, tomato paste, sugar, and thyme sprigs. Season to taste with salt and pepper.

❖ Put on the lid and cook on Low for 6–8 hours. The vegetables should be soft, but not mushy. Remove the thyme sprigs and sprinkle with the extra fresh thyme leaves and capers. Serve warm or at room temperature.

slow-cooked vegetable casserole

serves 4

1½ cups (10 oz/300 g) fresh or frozen lima beans

1½ cups (10 oz/300 g) fresh or frozen corn kernels

½ cup (1 oz/30 g) chopped green (spring) onion

½ cup (2½ oz/75 g) finely chopped celery

1 small red bell pepper (capsicum), chopped

1 red chile, seeded and chopped

½ cup (4 fl oz/125 ml) each
milk and light (single) cream

1 tablespoon butter, chopped

salt and ground black pepper

¼ cup (½ oz/15 g) chopped chives

❖ Put the beans, corn, green onion, celery, bell pepper,
and chile in the slow cooker and stir well to combine.
Pour on the milk and cream, dot with butter,
and season to taste with salt and pepper.

❖ Put on the lid and cook on Low
for 5–7 hours. Stir in the chives
and serve hot.

238

succotash

candied yams

serves 6–8

*5 yams or sweet potatoes, unpeeled,
about 4 lb (2 kg) total weight*

TOPPING

*1 cup (7 oz/220 g)
firmly packed
dark brown sugar*

*½ cup (4 oz/125 g)
unsalted butter,
at room temperature*

*½ cup (2 oz/60 g)
finely chopped walnuts*

*1 teaspoon pumpkin
pie spice (mixed spice), or
½ teaspoon ground cinnamon
and ¼ teaspoon each ground
nutmeg and allspice*

❖ Preheat the oven to 425°F (210°C/Gas Mark 5). Pierce each yam all over with a fork, wrap individually in aluminum foil, and place on a baking sheet. Bake the yams for about 1 hour, or until tender when pierced with a sharp knife.

❖ Remove the yams from the oven, and reduce the oven temperature to 400°F (200°C/Gas Mark 5). Unwrap the yams immediately and let cool. Using your fingers and a sharp knife, peel the yams and cut crosswise into slices 1 inch (2.5 cm) thick.

❖ For the topping, combine the brown sugar in a bowl with the butter, walnuts, and spice. Using a fork or your fingertips, mix until coarse and crumbly.

❖ Lightly butter an 8-inch (20-cm) square baking dish. Arrange half the yam slices in a single layer in the prepared dish. Sprinkle evenly with half the topping. Layer the remaining yam slices on top and sprinkle with the remaining topping. Place the baking dish on a baking sheet and bake for 15–20 minutes, or until the topping melts and is bubbling.

❖ Spoon onto warmed plates and serve immediately.

bean and sweet potato
burritos

serves 4

1 tablespoon vegetable oil

1 large yellow onion, thinly sliced

1 green bell pepper (capsicum), seeded and finely chopped

2 cloves garlic, finely chopped

1 large green chile, seeded and diced

1 tablespoon chili powder

1 teaspoon ground cumin

1 teaspoon dried oregano leaves

2 medium sweet potatoes, peeled and cut into ½ inch (1 cm) cubes

1 cup (6½ oz/200 g) frozen or fresh corn kernels

1 can (14 oz/440 g) kidney beans

four 10-inch (25-cm) flour tortillas

1 cup (4 oz/125 g) shredded Cheddar or Monterey Jack cheese

❖ Heat the oil in a large frying pan and cook the onion, bell pepper, garlic, and green chile for 3–4 minutes. Stir in the chili powder, ground cumin, and oregano and cook for 1 minute more.

❖ In the slow cooker, layer half the sweet potato then half the onion mixture, corn, and drained beans. Repeat the layers. Put on the lid and cook on Low for 5–6 hours, or until the sweet potato is tender.

❖ Preheat the oven to 350°F (180°C/ Gas Mark 4). Divide the mixture evenly among the tortillas and scatter with shredded cheese. Fold to enclose the filling and place in a greased baking pan. Cover with foil and bake for 25–30 minutes. Serve hot.

vegetable terrine
with tomato sauce

serves 6

TOMATO LAYER

1/4 cup (2 oz/60 g) unsalted butter

2 yellow onions, finely chopped

4 medium tomatoes, peeled, seeded, and chopped

2 cloves garlic, finely chopped

2 tablespoons chopped basil

3 tablespoons tomato paste

1 teaspoon chili powder

salt and ground black pepper

1 whole egg, plus 1 egg yolk

LEEK LAYER

1/3 cup (3 oz/90 g) unsalted butter

3 leeks, thinly sliced

2 cloves garlic, finely chopped

1/2 cup (1/2 oz/15 g) chopped parsley

salt and ground black pepper

1 whole egg, plus 1 egg yolk

TO ASSEMBLE

12 large cabbage leaves, blanched briefly in boiling water and refreshed in cold water

1 bunch asparagus, blanched briefly in boiling water and refreshed in cold water

2 red bell peppers (capsicums), roasted, skinned, and seeded

6 yellow squash, thinly sliced, blanched briefly in boiling water, and refreshed in cold water

TO SERVE

about 2 cups (16 fl oz/500 ml) Tomato Sauce (page 247)

vegetable terrine with tomato sauce

❖ For the tomato layer, melt the butter in a large, heavy-based, nonreactive pan. Add the onion, cover, and cook on low heat for 20 minutes. Drain the tomatoes and add to the onion. Cook, stirring often, for 20 minutes. Add the garlic, basil, tomato paste, chili powder, and salt and pepper to taste, and cook for 15 minutes, or until the mixture is very thick. Cool to room temperature. Whisk the egg and egg yolk into the tomato mixture. Cover and refrigerate until very cool. (This can be done up to a day ahead.)

❖ For the leek layer, melt the butter in a heavy-based pan. Add the leeks, cover, and cook on low heat for 30 minutes—do not let the leeks brown. Add the garlic, parsley, and salt and pepper to taste, and cook, uncovered, for another 10 minutes. Cool to room temperature. Beat the egg and yolk together in a small bowl. Stir into the leek mixture. Cover and refrigerate until very cool. (This can be done up to a day ahead.)

❖ Preheat the oven to 375°F (190°C/Gas Mark 4). To assemble the terrine, drain the cabbage, asparagus, bell peppers, and squash; pat dry with paper towels. Lightly butter a 9- x 5- x 3-inch (23- x 13- x 7.5-cm) terrine or loaf pan. Trim the heavy ribs from the cabbage leaves. Line the pan with cabbage leaves, overlapping them and allowing the tops to hang out over the edges of the pan. Reserve 2 or 3 cabbage leaves for the top.

❖ Stir the cooled leek and tomato mixtures. Smooth half the tomato mixture on the bottom of the lined terrine. Layer the asparagus on top, then add all of the leek mixture, smoothing the surface. Layer the roasted bell peppers on top and cover with

vegetable terrine with tomato sauce

the rest of the tomato mixture. Arrange the squash slices on top. Fold the overhanging cabbage leaves over the top, tucking any excess down the sides of the terrine.

❖ Wrap the terrine in aluminum foil, place in a large baking pan, and pour in boiling water to reach halfway up the sides of the terrine. Bake in the center of the oven for 2 hours, or until the terrine is firm to the touch. Remove from the water and unwrap. Cool for 15 minutes. Set a weight over the terrine and cool completely. Remove the weight, cover the terrine, and refrigerate. To unmold, dip the pan briefly in hot water and run a thin knife around the sides, then invert. Serve with tomato sauce.

tomato sauce

5 medium tomatoes, peeled and seeded

2 tablespoons red wine vinegar

dash of hot-pepper sauce

1/2 teaspoon chili powder (optional)

salt and ground black pepper, to taste

1/3 cup (3 fl oz/100 ml) olive oil

❖ Process all the ingredients, except the oil, together in a food processor until smooth. Add the oil in a slow, steady stream and process until completely combined. Chill in the refrigerator. Just before serving, adjust the seasoning.

makes about 2 cups (16 fl oz/500 ml)

baked
winter squash

Use any flavorsome small
winter squash, such as
Danish, buttercup, butternut,
or pumpkin. Some squashes
will have more pulp than
others, in which case you
may need to use both
shells for serving.

1 small winter squash, 1½–2 lb (750 g–1 kg)

1 cup (8 fl oz/250 ml) vegetable stock

¼ cup (2 oz/60 g) unsalted butter

½ yellow onion, finely chopped

3 tablespoons chopped fresh parsley

1 teaspoon dried marjoram

2 egg yolks

¼ cup (2 fl oz/60 ml) heavy (double) cream

¼ cup (1 oz/30 g) freshly grated Parmesan cheese

salt and ground pepper

◈ Preheat the oven to 375°F (190°C/Gas Mark 4).

◈ Cut the squash in half lengthwise. Place cut side down in a baking dish. Pour the stock into the dish. Place in the oven and bake for about 45 minutes, or until tender. To test, pierce the flesh with a fork.

◈ Melt half the butter in a frying pan over medium heat. Add the onion and cook, stirring, for about 2 minutes, or until soft. Add 2 tablespoons of the parsley and the marjoram and cook, stirring, for 1 minute. Remove from the heat and set aside. Scoop out and discard the seeds and fibers from the baked squash halves. Scoop out the pulp, reserving one or both of the squash shells. Place the pulp in a food processor fitted with a metal blade. Add the remaining butter and the egg yolks and process to blend. Add the cream, cheese, and onion mixture, and again process to blend. Season to taste with salt and pepper.

◈ Spoon the squash mixture evenly into the squash shell(s) and place in a baking dish. Bake for 15–20 minutes, or until the top is golden.

◈ Sprinkle the remaining parsley over the top and serve hot, spooned directly from the shell.

baked onions

serves 4

4 red (Spanish) onions,
unpeeled

4 sprigs fresh rosemary or basil

¼ cup (2 fl oz/60 ml) olive oil

2 tablespoons red wine vinegar

1½ tablespoons
balsamic vinegar

1 tablespoon brown sugar

¾ cup (6 fl oz/190 ml)
vegetable or chicken stock

salt and ground pepper

❖ Preheat the oven to 375°F (190°C/Gas Mark 4). Using a sharp knife, cut a thin slice off the base of each onion so the onions will sit upright. Cut a thin slice from the top of each onion and then cut a small slit ½ inch (1 cm) deep in the center. Insert a rosemary or basil sprig into each slit.

❖ Place the onions in a small baking dish. Combine the olive oil, vinegars, sugar, and stock in a small bowl. Pour into the bottom of the dish and baste the onions with the liquid. Bake, basting a few times with the juices in the pan, for 1–1½ hours, or until the onions are soft when pierced with the point of a sharp knife.

❖ Before serving, split the skins with a sharp knife and remove. Season the onions to taste with salt and pepper.

italian casserole
of vegetables

serves 4

3 fl oz (100 ml) olive oil

2 potatoes, sliced

2 onions, sliced

2 carrots, scraped and sliced

1 eggplant (aubergine), sliced

1 bell pepper (capsicum), sliced

1 rib (stick) celery, sliced

2 tablespoons shelled peas

4 ripe tomatoes, sliced

salt and ground pepper

½ cup (4 fl oz/125 ml) chicken stock

2 cloves garlic, finely chopped

1 tablespoon chopped fresh parsley

❖ Coat a cooktop-to-table casserole with 1 tablespoon of the oil. Add the potatoes, onions, carrots, eggplant, bell pepper, celery, peas, and tomatoes in layers, seasoning each layer lightly with salt and pepper.

❖ Mix the remaining oil with the stock and garlic. Pour over the vegetables. Cover the casserole and cook over very low heat for about 1 hour.

❖ Scatter the parsley over the vegetables and serve the vegetables straight from the casserole onto individual plates.

oven-roasted potatoes
with rosemary and garlic

serves 4

All over Italy, trattorias prepare potatoes in this simple manner. For the best flavor, select yellow-fleshed potatoes, such as Finnish Yellow or Yukon Gold, or white-fleshed Maine potatoes.

¼ cup (2 fl oz/60 ml) olive oil

12 large cloves garlic, lightly crushed

1½ lb (750 g) yellow-fleshed potatoes, peeled and cut into 1-inch (2.5-cm) pieces

8 sprigs fresh rosemary, or to taste

salt and ground black pepper

✧ Preheat the oven to 425°F (210°C/Gas Mark 5).

✧ Heat the olive oil and garlic in a metal baking pan over low heat for 1–2 minutes, or until the garlic flavor is released into the hot oil. Remove from the heat.

✧ Meanwhile, fill a saucepan three-fourths full of water and bring to the boil. Put the potato pieces in the boiling water for 10 seconds, then drain and immediately transfer the potatoes to the baking pan holding the garlic and oil, leaving a little water still dripping from the potato pieces. (This step helps to prevent the potato pieces from breaking up during roasting.)

✧ Sprinkle the rosemary sprigs over the potatoes. Toss gently to coat the potatoes and rosemary thoroughly with the oil. Spread the potatoes out in a single layer in the baking pan.

✧ Place the pan in the center of the oven and immediately reduce the heat to 375°F (190°C/Gas Mark 4). Roast, stirring 2 or 3 times for even browning, for about 1 hour, or until the potatoes are tender when pierced with a fork and golden brown with crisp edges. Season to taste with salt and pepper.

✧ Transfer to a warmed serving dish and serve immediately.

slow-baked tomatoes

serves 6 as an accompaniment

*2 lb (1 kg) plum (Roma)
tomatoes, halved lengthwise*

2 tablespoons olive oil

1 tablespoon sugar

3 teaspoons thyme leaves

ground black pepper

❖ Preheat the oven to 300°F (150°C/Gas Mark 2).

❖ Place the tomatoes, cut sides up, in an oiled baking dish. Drizzle with the oil, sprinkle with the sugar, then scatter the thyme and pepper on top.

❖ Bake the tomatoes for 1¼–1½ hours, or until they are soft and lightly browned around the edges. Serve warm or at room temperature.

potato and spinach terrine

serves 6

3 eggs

*1¼ cups (10 fl oz/315 ml)
sour cream*

*about 13 oz (400 g) spinach,
blanched, well drained,
and finely chopped*

2 tablespoons chopped chives

1 tablespoon finely chopped dill

*⅔ cup (2½ oz/75 g) freshly
grated Parmesan cheese*

salt and ground pepper

*2 lb (1 kg) all-purpose
potatoes, peeled and
thinly sliced*

❖ Preheat the oven to 350°F (180°C/Gas Mark 4).

❖ Beat the eggs and sour cream together in a bowl.
Add the spinach, chives, dill, and cheese, and mix
thoroughly. Season to taste with salt and pepper.

❖ Grease an 8- x 5-inch (20- x 13-cm) loaf pan (or
use a nonstick pan), and spread some of the spinach
mixture to cover the base. Cover with a layer of sliced
potatoes. Repeat the layers until all the ingredients are
used, finishing with the spinach mixture. Cover the pan
tightly with buttered aluminum foil. Place the loaf pan
in a roasting pan with enough hot water to come
halfway up the sides.

❖ Cook for 1¼ hours. Remove the foil and cook for
15 minutes longer. Serve hot or cold.

zucchini, carrot, and barley pilaf

serves 4–6

Barley's nutty flavor makes
an interesting change from
rice in this delicious pilaf.
You could also make it with
half rice and half barley.

½ oz (15 g) dried porcini mushrooms

1 tablespoon vegetable oil

1 yellow onion, chopped

2 cloves garlic, chopped

½ teaspoon dried oregano leaves

2 cups (16 fl oz/500 ml) vegetable stock

1 cup (7 oz/220 g) pearl barley, rinsed and drained

salt and ground black pepper

1 large carrot, shredded

2 medium zucchini (courgettes)

½ cup (½ oz/15 g) chopped fresh parsley

❖ Grease a 6-cup (1½-qt/1.5-l) heatproof soufflé dish or bowl that will fit into the slow cooker.

❖ Make foil handles to aid removal of the dish after cooking by cutting three 18- x 2-inch (45- x 5-cm) strips of heavy-duty foil or regular foil folded to a double thickness. Crisscross the foil strips in a spoke design over the base and up the sides of the slow cooker.

❖ Soak the porcini mushrooms in ½ cup (4 fl oz/125 ml) hot water for 5 minutes. Chop the mushrooms finely and reserve the soaking liquid.

❖ Heat the oil in a large frying pan and cook the onion and garlic for 2–3 minutes. Add the dried oregano leaves, the porcini mushrooms, and their liquid, and stir over high heat until the liquid has evaporated. Add the stock and barley. Season to taste with salt and pepper. Transfer to the prepared dish or bowl. Stir in the shredded carrot.

❖ Shred the zucchini and pat or squeeze out the excess moisture with paper towels or a clean tea towel. Stir the zucchini and parsley into the barley mixture. Cover securely with foil.

❖ Lower the soufflé dish into the slow cooker and pour in enough boiling water around the dish to come halfway up the sides. Put on the lid and cook on Low for 6–8 hours, or until the barley is tender. Use the foil handles to aid in the removal of the dish. Serve hot from the soufflé dish.

potato gratin

serves 4

3 tablespoons butter

1 small egg

salt and ground black pepper

freshly grated nutmeg

1/2 cup (4 fl oz/125 ml) milk

1/2 cup (4 fl oz/125 ml)
light (single) cream

1 lb (500 g) all-purpose
potatoes, peeled and
thinly sliced

3/4 cup (3 oz/90 g) shredded
Gruyère cheese

❖ Preheat the oven to 350°F (180°C/Gas Mark 4).

❖ Lightly grease a shallow ovenproof dish with a little of the butter.

❖ Beat the egg, salt, pepper, and nutmeg together in a mixing bowl. Whisk in the milk and cream.

❖ Place half the potatoes in the dish and sprinkle with half the cheese. Pour over 1/4 cup (2 fl oz/60 ml) of the milk mixture. Add the rest of the potatoes and milk mixture. Top with the remaining cheese and dot with the remaining butter.

❖ Bake for 40–50 minutes, or until the potatoes are tender and the top is golden brown.

oven-baked
french fries

serves 6

12 small potatoes, unpeeled,
sliced into French fries

½ cup (4 fl oz/125 ml) olive oil,
or olive oil spray

sea salt

❖ Preheat the oven to 400°F (200°C/Gas Mark 5).

❖ Lightly spray or brush a baking sheet with olive oil.
Arrange the fries on the baking sheet. Spray or brush
the potato surfaces with olive oil.

❖ Bake for 50–60 minutes, or until the French fries are
crisp and golden.

❖ Serve immediately, sprinkled with flakes of sea salt.

eggplant _purée_

serves 3–4

Try this delicious eggplant purée as a healthy, low-fat alternative to butter on savory sandwiches.

2 globe eggplants (aubergines), about 8 oz (250 g) each

1 tablespoon extra-virgin olive oil

$\frac{1}{2}$ tablespoon lemon juice

2–3 pinches ground cumin

1 small clove garlic, crushed and chopped

salt

◈ Preheat the oven to 475°F (230°C/Gas Mark 6).

◈ Pierce each eggplant 2 or 3 times with a knife so they will not burst while cooking.

◈ Place the eggplants on a rack in the hot oven, with a pan below to catch the drippings. Cook for about 45 minutes, or until eggplants are shriveled. Remove them from the oven and let cool for 20 minutes.

◈ Peel the eggplants, reserving the pulp. Mash pulp coarsely with a fork, gradually adding the oil, lemon juice, cumin, garlic, and salt. (Increase the amount of oil and decrease the lemon juice according to taste.)

◈ Serve the purée cold, with crusty bread or slices of toast, along with other antipasto dishes such as tapenade (black olive paste), anchovy fillets in oil, and thin strips of grilled bell pepper (capsicum). It may also be used to accompany grilled fish and cold roast meats.

recipe variations

If you add tahini paste, lemon juice, and garlic to the eggplant purée, you will have a spread or dip that is similar to the delicious Middle Eastern dish called baba ghanoush. White tahini paste is less bitter than the darker version, which incorporates the hulls of the sesame seeds and has quite a high oxalic acid content. Use whichever you prefer.

corn and bell pepper
pudding

serves 4–6

3 large eggs

½ cup (2½ oz/75 g) all-purpose (plain) flour

½ teaspoon sweet paprika

¼ teaspoon cayenne pepper

¼ cup (2 oz/60 g) butter, melted

½ cup (4 fl oz/125 ml) full-cream milk

½ cup (4 fl oz/125 ml) heavy (double) cream

2 cups (13 oz/400 g) fresh corn kernels

3 green (spring) onions, finely chopped

1 small red bell pepper (capsicum), seeded and chopped

1 cup (1 oz/30 g) chopped parsley

salt and ground black pepper

◈ Grease a 6-cup (1½-qt/1.5-l) heatproof soufflé dish or bowl that will fit into the slow cooker.

◈ Make foil handles to aid removal of the dish after cooking by cutting three 18- x 2-inch (45- x 5-cm) strips of heavy-duty foil or regular foil folded to a double thickness. Crisscross the foil strips in a spoke design over the base and up the sides of the slow cooker.

◈ Beat the eggs lightly in a large bowl. Sift the flour, paprika, and cayenne pepper into a small bowl. Whisk the flour mixture into the egg mixture and beat until a smooth batter forms. Add the melted butter, milk, and cream.

◈ Stir in the corn, spring onions, bell pepper, and parsley. Season to taste with salt and pepper. Transfer to the prepared dish and cover the top firmly with foil.

◈ Lower the soufflé dish into the slow cooker and pour in enough boiling water around the dish to come halfway up the sides. Put on the lid and cook on Low for 6–8 hours. The pudding is cooked when a knife inserted in the center comes out clean. Use the foil handles to aid in the removal of the dish.

◈ Rest for 5 minutes, then serve while hot. This dish is excellent with roast chicken.

slow-cooked
desserts

baked
fruity apples

serves 4

4 medium cooking apples

4 fresh or dried dates,
seeded and chopped

2 dried apricots, chopped

8 raisins

½ teaspoon ground cinnamon

¼ teaspoon ground nutmeg
or mixed spice

2 tablespoons softened butter

½ cup (4 oz/125 g)
superfine (caster) sugar

1 cup (8 fl oz/250 ml) water

custard or ice cream, to serve

◈ Using an apple corer, remove the core from each apple. Make a shallow slit horizontally around the circumference of each apple.

◈ Combine the chopped dates, apricots, raisins, and spices in a small bowl, and mix in the butter with your fingertips. Push a fourth of the mixture into the hollow center of each apple. Place in the slow cooker, leaving a little space between the apples.

◈ Combine the sugar and water in a small saucepan. Stir to dissolve, then simmer for 2–3 minutes. Pour the hot syrup over the apples. Put on the lid and cook on Low for 5–6 hours. Insert a knife into the apples to check for doneness.

◈ Serve hot or warm with custard or ice cream.

bread-and-butter pudding
with apricots and currants

serves 4–6

The ultimate nursery pudding is here given a fruity new treatment, highlighted by the addition of a delicious layer of apricots and currants.

6 thin slices fruit bread, crusts removed

1/4 cup (2 oz/60 g) softened butter

1 can (15 oz/470 g) apricot halves, drained

2 tablespoons currants

3 eggs

1/3 cup (2 1/2 oz/75 g) superfine (caster) sugar

1 teaspoon vanilla extract (essence)

2 cups (16 fl oz/500 ml) full-cream milk, warmed

grated nutmeg, for sprinkling

✥ Grease a 5-cup (40-fl oz/1.25-l) heatproof soufflé dish or bowl that will fit into the slow cooker.

✥ Make foil handles to aid removal of the dish after cooking by cutting three 18- x 2-inch (45- x 5-cm) strips of heavy-duty foil or regular foil folded to a double thickness. Crisscross the foil strips in a spoke design over the base and up the sides of the slow cooker.

✥ Butter the bread on one side and cut each slice in half. Line the prepared dish with half the bread slices, placing them buttered side down. Scatter the apricots and currants over the bread. Arrange the remaining buttered bread over the fruit layer.

✥ Whisk the eggs in a bowl with the sugar and vanilla, then whisk in the warmed milk. Pour over the bread mixture and sprinkle the top with little nutmeg.

✥ Cover the dish securely with buttered foil. Lower the dish into the slow cooker and pour in enough boiling water around the dish to come halfway up the sides. Put on the lid and cook on Low for 4–6 hours, or until the custard has set. (Test by inserting a knife into the center of the custard; if it comes out clean, the custard is cooked.) Use the foil handles to aid in the removal of the dish. Serve warm with custard or cream, if desired.

fresh peach tart

serves 8–10

FILLING

3½ lb (1.75 kg) ripe, but firm, yellow
peaches, peeled, pitted, and chopped

½ cup (4 oz/125 g) sugar
or ⅓ cup (3½ oz/105 g) honey, or to taste

½ cup (4 fl oz/125 ml) dry Italian
white wine

PASTRY

¼ cup (1 oz/30 g) slivered
blanched almonds

½ cup (4 oz/125 g) sugar

2 cups (10 oz/315 g) all-purpose
(plain) flour

pinch of baking soda (bicarbonate of soda)

pinch of salt

2 extra-large eggs

2 teaspoons vanilla extract (essence)

¾ teaspoon finely grated lemon zest

¾ teaspoon finely grated orange zest

⅓ cup (2½ fl oz/80 ml) mild-flavored
olive oil

1 teaspoon distilled white vinegar

◈ Toss the peaches in a bowl with the sugar or honey; let stand for 1 hour. Transfer to a saucepan, add the wine, and bring to the boil. Reduce the heat to low and simmer, uncovered, for about 10 minutes, or until soft. Drain, reserving the liquid for another purpose, and let cool.

◈ For the pastry, combine the almonds and a little of the sugar in a food processor fitted with a metal blade and process until finely ground. Add the remaining sugar, the flour, baking soda, and salt, and pulse briefly until blended.

◈ Whisk the eggs in a small bowl with the vanilla and citrus zests; set aside. Turn the food processor on and pour in the oil, then the vinegar, and finally the egg mixture, mixing for only a few seconds until a ball of dough forms. Divide into 2 portions, one twice as large as the other. Cover and refrigerate the smaller portion.

◈ Preheat the oven to 425°F (210°C/Gas Mark 5). Place the large dough portion between 2 sheets of floured waxed paper. Roll into a round about 11 inches (28 cm) in diameter and ⅛ inch (3 mm) thick. Peel off one piece of paper and transfer the round, paper side up, to a tart pan with a removable base, 9 inches (23 cm) in diameter and 1¼ inches (3 cm) deep. Remove paper and press pastry into pan; trim off the overhang. Spread filling over the pastry.

◈ Roll out the remaining dough portion to a round 10 inches (25 cm) in diameter. Using a fluted or plain pastry wheel, cut into strips ½ inch (1 cm) wide. Make a decorative lattice with the strips, trimming off any overhang, and pressing the strips against the rim to secure them.

◈ Reduce heat to 375°F (190°C/Gas Mark 4) and bake tart on a baking sheet in center of oven for 25–30 minutes. Rotate tart to ensure even browning and reduce heat to 300°F (150°C/Gas Mark 2). Bake for 20–25 minutes longer, or until crust is golden and filling puffs up. Serve cool.

rhubarb with almond sponge

serves 4–6

1 lb (500 g) rhubarb, cut into
1-inch (2.5-cm) slices

¼ cup (2 oz/60 g) superfine
(caster) sugar

½ cup (4 oz/125 g) butter,
softened

½ cup (3½ oz/100 g)
brown sugar

1 teaspoon almond
extract (essence)

2 eggs, lightly beaten

1¼ cups (6½ oz/220 g)
self-raising flour

1 teaspoon baking powder

¼ cup (1½ oz/45 g)
almond meal (ground almonds)

◈ Lightly grease the inside of the slow cooker. Spread the rhubarb evenly over the base and sprinkle with the superfine sugar.

◈ Using an electric mixer, cream the butter, brown sugar, and almond extract in a medium bowl. Beat until thick and creamy. Add the beaten egg in three batches, beating well after each addition.

◈ Sift the flour and baking powder together. Gently fold the sifted flour mixture and the almond meal into the butter mixture. Spoon evenly over the rhubarb and smooth the surface. Cover with a round of buttered greaseproof paper cut to fit.

◈ Put on the lid and cook on High for 3–4 hours, or until the sponge is set and firm to the touch. Serve hot or warm with custard or cream, if desired.

creamy rice pudding

serves 4–6

2½ cups (15 oz/470 g)
cooked white
short-grain rice

½ cup (2½ oz/75 g)
currants

¼ cup (2 oz/60 g)
brown sugar

1 cup (8 fl oz/250 ml)
full-cream milk

½ cup (4 fl oz/125 ml)
cream

2 tablespoons
(1 oz/30 g) butter,
chopped

1 teaspoon nutmeg

◈ Grease a 5-cup (40-fl oz/1.25-l) heatproof soufflé dish or bowl that will fit into the slow cooker.

◈ Make foil handles to aid removal of the dish after cooking by cutting three 18- x 2-inch (45- x 5-cm) strips of heavy-duty foil or regular foil folded to a double thickness. Crisscross the foil strips in a spoke design over the base and up the sides of the slow cooker.

◈ Place the rice and currants in the prepared dish. Mix the sugar, milk, and cream together in a medium bowl. Pour into the dish and sprinkle with the chopped butter and nutmeg.

◈ Cover the dish securely with buttered foil. Lower the dish into the slow cooker and pour in enough boiling water around the dish to come halfway up the sides. Put on the lid and cook on Low for 4–6 hours, or High for 1–2 hours, or until the custard is creamy. Serve hot, warm, or cool.

spiced baked pears

serves 6

Gleaming baked pears are a popular choice in any dessert selection. For another version of this time-honored dessert, peel the top third of the skin and sprinkle with cinnamon.

FILLING

¼ cup (1 oz/30 g) pecan halves

⅓ cup (3 oz/90 g) unsalted butter, chilled, cut into small pieces

⅓ cup (2½ oz/75 g) firmly packed light or dark brown sugar

2 tablespoons coarsely chopped dried apricots

2 tablespoons golden raisins (sultanas)

½ teaspoon ground cinnamon

⅛ teaspoon ground cloves

¼ teaspoon ground allspice

⅛ teaspoon ground nutmeg

6 ripe, but firm, pears

1 cup (8 fl oz/250 ml) apple juice

✥ Preheat the oven to 350°F (180°C/Gas Mark 4).

✥ For the filling, spread the pecan halves on a baking sheet and bake for 5–7 minutes, or until lightly toasted. Remove from the oven, let cool, and chop coarsely. Set aside. Increase the oven temperature to 400°F (200°C/Gas Mark 5).

✥ Combine the butter and sugar in a small bowl. Using your fingertips or a wooden spoon, mix to a paste-like consistency. Stir in the toasted nuts, apricots, raisins, cinnamon, cloves, allspice, and nutmeg. Set aside.

✥ Cut a thin slice off the bottom of each pear so that it will stand upright. Working from the stem ends and using a sharp knife, core the pears without cutting through the bottoms.

✥ Using a small spoon, stuff the mixture into the cored pears, dividing it equally among them. Smooth the tops and cover just the filling with aluminum foil.

✥ Place the pears in a 9- x 13-inch (23- x 33-cm) baking dish. Pour the apple juice into the dish. Bake, basting the pears with the dish juices every 15 minutes, for 30–45 minutes, or until the pears are tender when pierced with a knife.

✥ Transfer the baked pears to a platter or individual serving dishes and serve immediately, with some of the juices and cream, if desired.

apple crisp
with dried cranberries

serves 6

TOPPING

1 cup (4 oz/125 g) coarsely chopped pecans

¾ cup (4 oz/125 g) all-purpose (plain) flour

½ teaspoon ground cinnamon

¼ teaspoon ground nutmeg

¼ teaspoon ground allspice

⅛ teaspoon ground cloves

pinch of salt

¾ cup (2½ oz/75 g) quick-cooking rolled oats

½ cup (4 oz/125 g) granulated (white) sugar

½ cup (3½ oz/100 g) firmly packed light brown sugar

¾ cup (6 oz/185 g) unsalted butter, chilled, cut into small pieces

FILLING

8 Golden Delicious apples, about 2½ lb (1.25 kg) total weight

3 tablespoons fresh lemon juice

½ cup (2 oz/60 g) dried cranberries

❖ Preheat the oven to 350°F (180°C/Gas Mark 4). Butter a 9- x 12-inch (23- x 30-cm) oval baking dish.

❖ For the topping, spread the pecans on a baking sheet and bake for 5–7 minutes, or until lightly toasted. Remove from the oven and let cool.

❖ Combine the flour, cinnamon, nutmeg, allspice, cloves, and salt in a large bowl. Add the toasted pecans, rolled oats, granulated sugar, brown sugar, and butter. Using your fingertips, rub the mixture together until it resembles coarse crumbs. Set aside.

❖ For the filling, peel, halve, and core the apples, then cut lengthwise into slices ½ inch (1 cm) thick. Place in a bowl, immediately add the lemon juice and dried cranberries, and toss to coat with the juice. Pour the filling into the prepared dish, leveling the surface. Sprinkle the topping evenly over the fruit, pressing down on it lightly and leaving about ¼ inch (6 mm) space between the topping and the sides of the pan.

❖ Bake for 40–45 minutes, or until the topping is golden brown and bubbling, covering the top with aluminum foil if the crust begins to overbrown.

❖ Transfer to a rack and let cool for 15 minutes before serving with cream or ice cream, if desired.

fresh peach and rhubarb pie

serves 6–8

Pastry for Double-crust Pie (made in a food processor) (page 277)

FILLING
3 rhubarb stalks, cut into ½-inch (1-cm) pieces (about 2 cups/8 oz/250 g)

6–7 peaches, peeled or unpeeled, cored and cut into slices ½ inch (1 cm) thick (about 4 cups/1½ lb/750 g)

3 tablespoons fresh lemon juice

¾ cup (6 oz/185 g) sugar

¼ teaspoon ground nutmeg

½ teaspoon ground cinnamon

⅓ cup (2 oz/60 g) all-purpose (plain) flour

1 egg, beaten with 1 tablespoon water

❖ Prepare the pastry as directed in the recipe.

❖ For the filling, combine the rhubarb, peaches, lemon juice, sugar, nutmeg, cinnamon, and flour in a large bowl and toss to mix. On a lightly floured work surface, roll out the larger portion of pastry to a round about 11 inches (28 cm) in diameter. Gently ease the pastry into a deep 9-inch (23-cm) pie plate and press into the plate, trmming off any overhang. Brush the pie crust with the egg-and-water mixture. Spoon the filling into the crust.

❖ Preheat oven to 425°F (210°C/Gas Mark 5).

❖ On the lightly floured work surface, roll out the remaining pastry into a 10-inch (25-cm) round. Using a fluted or plain pastry wheel or a sharp knife, cut the round into strips ½ inch (1 cm) wide. Make a decorative lattice by laying rows of pastry strips ¾ inch (2 cm) apart across the top of the pie. Press the ends firmly to the edge of the crust and trim off any overhang. Lay the remaining strips in the opposite direction, again pressing them firmly to the edge and trimming off any overhang. Flute or crimp the edge decoratively. Brush the pastry edge and strips with the egg/water mixture.

✣ Bake the pie on a baking sheet for 10 minutes. Reduce the heat to 350°F (180°C/Gas Mark 4) and continue baking for 35–45 minutes, or until golden brown and bubbling. (Check the pie during baking and cover the edges with aluminum foil if the crust begins to overbrown.)

✣ Transfer the pie to a rack and allow to cool for 20 minutes before serving. Serve warm or cool, with custard or ice cream, if desired.

pastry for double-crust pie

(made in a food processor)

2 cups (10 oz/315 g) all-purpose (plain) flour, plus flour for rolling

½ teaspoon salt

½ cup (4 oz/125 g) unsalted butter, chilled, cut into small pieces

3 tablespoons vegetable shortening, chilled

1 egg yolk

1 tablespoon fresh lemon juice

5 tablespoons (3 fl oz/80 ml) ice water

✣ Combine flour and salt in food processor fitted with a metal blade. Process briefly to blend. Add the butter and shortening and process for 5–10 seconds, or until mixture resembles coarse crumbs. With the motor running, gradually add the egg yolk, lemon juice, and just enough of the ice water for the dough to come together and hold a shape when pressed. Remove the dough from the processor, divide into 2 pieces, one slightly larger than the other, and flatten into 2 thick disks. Wrap the disks in plastic wrap and refrigerate for 1–24 hours.

harvest apple pie

serves 6–8

Pastry for Double-crust Pie (page 295)

FILLING
2 lb (1 kg) Golden Delicious, Gravenstein,
or Granny Smith apples, peeled, cored, and
cut into slices ½ inch (1 cm) thick

1¼ cups (10 oz/315 g) sugar

1½ teaspoons fresh lemon juice

1 teaspoon vanilla extract (essence)

¼ teaspoon ground nutmeg

¼ teaspoon ground cinnamon

⅛ teaspoon salt

2½ tablespoons all-purpose (plain) flour

5 tablespoons (2½ oz/75 g) chilled unsalted
butter, cut into pieces

1 egg

1 tablespoon water

◈ Prepare the pastry dough as directed and refrigerate for 1 hour.

◈ Combine the apples, sugar, lemon juice, vanilla, nutmeg, cinnamon, and salt in a bowl. Toss until the apples are evenly coated. Add the flour and toss again to coat evenly. Cover and refrigerate until needed.

◈ Preheat the oven to 375°F (190°C/Gas Mark 4). Lightly butter and flour a 9-inch (23-cm) pie pan and tap out the excess flour.

◈ Using a heavy rolling pin and working on a lightly floured surface, roll out the larger portion of pastry into a round 12 inches (30 cm) in diameter and about ⅛ inch (3 mm) thick. Carefully transfer the pastry to the prepared pan and press gently into the bottom and sides.

◈ Transfer the apple mixture to the pastry-lined pan. Dot the top with pieces of butter.

◈ Roll out the remaining pastry into a round about 10 inches (25 cm) in diameter. Whisk the egg and water together in a small bowl. Using a pastry brush, brush the edge of the bottom pastry shell with a light coating of the egg mixture. Lay the second pastry round on top and, using scissors, trim away all but about ½ inch (1 cm) of the overhanging dough. Crimp the top and bottom edges together to seal and form a decorative rim. Cut a small slit in the top of the pie for a steam vent. Brush the top lightly with the egg mixture.

◈ Bake the pie on a baking sheet for 40–50 minutes, or until the crust is a rich golden brown. Remove from the oven and transfer to a rack to cool slightly. Serve warm or cool.

PASTRY

1¼ cups (6½ oz/220 g)
all-purpose (plain) flour

¼ cup (2 oz/60 g) sugar

½ cup (4 oz/125 g)
chilled butter

2 egg yolks, beaten

1 tablespoon iced water

DUMPLINGS

¼ cup (2 oz/60 g) sugar

¼ teaspoon
grated nutmeg

about 1¼ oz (40 g)
packaged cream cheese,
softened

6 plums, halved
and pitted

half-and-half (half
cream) or light
(single) cream, for
brushing and serving

❖ For the pastry, combine flour and sugar in a medium
mixing bowl. Cut in butter until the pieces are the size
of small peas. Stir the egg yolks and water together in a
small mixing bowl. Gradually stir egg mixture into flour
mixture. Gently knead the dough just until a ball forms.
Cover dough with plastic wrap and chill for 30–60 minutes.

❖ Combine sugar and nutmeg in a small bowl. Set aside.
In another small mixing bowl, beat the cream cheese and
3 tablespoons of the sugar mixture with an electric mixer
on medium speed until fluffy. Set aside.

❖ Preheat the oven to 375°F (190°C/Gas Mark 4). On a
lightly floured surface, roll the dough into an 18- x 12-inch
(45- x 30-cm) rectangle. Cut into six 6-inch (15-cm) squares.
For each dumpling, spread 2 teaspoons of cream cheese
mixture on the cut side of 6 plum halves. Top each with
another plum half and place in the center of a dough
square. Moisten the dough edges with water, fold the
corners to the center, and pinch to seal the edges.

❖ Place the dumplings in a shallow baking pan. Brush
with some of the half-and-half and sprinkle with the
remaining sugar mixture. Bake the dumplings for about
30 minutes, or until the plums are tender and the pastry
is golden. Serve warm with half-and-half or light cream.

plum dumplings

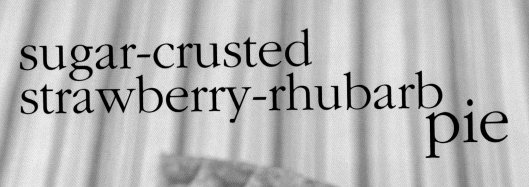

sugar-crusted strawberry-rhubarb pie

1¼ cups (10 oz/315 g) sugar

3 tablespoons quick-cooking tapioca

3 cups (13 oz/400 g) strawberries, sliced

2 cups (8 oz/250 g) fresh or thawed frozen unsweetened sliced rhubarb

½ teaspoon finely shredded orange zest

½ teaspoon ground cinnamon

¼ teaspoon ground nutmeg

¼ cup superfine (caster) sugar

Pastry for Double-crust Pie (page 295)

❖ Combine the sugar and tapioca in a large mixing bowl. Add the strawberries, rhubarb, orange zest, cinnamon, and nutmeg. Toss gently until the fruit is coated, then stand, stirring occasionally, for about 15 minutes, or until a syrup forms.

❖ Prepare the pastry as directed and set aside to rest. Preheat the oven to 375°F (190°C/Gas Mark 4). Divide the pastry in halves and roll out. Line a 9-inch (23-cm) pie plate with half the pastry. Stir the fruit mixture and transfer to pastry-lined pie plate. Place the remaining crust over the filling. Seal and crimp the edge and trim off even with rim. Cut slits in the top crust, brush with water, and sprinkle with sugar.

❖ To prevent overbrowning, cover the edge of the pie with foil. Bake for 25 minutes. Remove the foil and bake for 20–25 minutes more, or until the top is golden. Cool on a wire rack.

spiced pears
in red wine

serves 4

*2 cups (16 fl oz/500 ml)
red wine*

1 cup (8 oz/250 g) sugar

4 firm ripe pears

2 thin strips lemon zest

1 cinnamon stick

4 whole cloves

*purchased or homemade
custard, heavy (double)
cream, or yogurt,
to serve (optional)*

❖ Combine the wine and sugar in a small saucepan and stir over low heat until the sugar has dissolved.

❖ Peel the pears, leaving the stalks intact. Slice a little off the base of each pear to make them sit upright, if necessary. Arrange the pears in the slow cooker, allowing space between them.

❖ Pour the wine syrup over and add the lemon zest, cinnamon stick, and cloves. Put on the lid and cook on Low for 4–6 hours. Turn the pears occasionally to coat in the wine mixture so that they color evenly. To check for doneness, insert a knife or fine skewer into the pears.

❖ Serve hot or warm with some of the cooking liquid. Custard, heavy (double) cream, or yogurt makes a delicious accompaniment.

dried fruit compote

serves 4–6

1 cup (7 oz/220 g) whole pitted prunes

1 cup (6 oz/185 g) whole dried apricot halves

1 cup (3 oz/90 g) dried apple rings

½ cup (2 oz/60 g) raisins

½ cup (4 oz/125 g) superfine (caster) sugar

1½ cups (12 fl oz/375 ml) white wine

1 cup (8 fl oz/250 ml) water

shredded strips of lemon zest

2 whole cloves

½ teaspoon ground allspice

TO SERVE

heavy (double) cream, whipped

toasted flaked almonds

❖ Place all the fruit in the slow cooker and sprinkle with the sugar. Pour on the wine and water. Add the lemon zest, whole cloves, and allspice.

❖ Put on the lid and cook on Low for 3–4 hours. The fruit should be soft but not mushy. Remove the lemon zest and whole cloves.

❖ Serve warm or cold. Top with whipped cream and sprinkle with the toasted flaked almonds.

honey and nut tart

serves 10–12

PASTRY

Pastry for Single-crust Pie (page 291)

¼ cup (1 oz/30 g) ground pecans or walnuts

FILLING

2 eggs

½ cup (3½ oz/100 g) packed brown sugar

½ cup (5½ oz/175 g) honey

3 tablespoons (1½ oz/50 g) butter or margarine, melted

¼ teaspoon finely shredded orange zest

2 teaspoons orange liqueur (optional)

1 cup (5 oz/160 g) coarsely chopped unsalted mixed cocktail nuts or coarsely chopped unsalted nuts, such as pecans, peanuts, hazelnuts, macadamias, almonds, and/or walnuts

ORANGE WHIPPED CREAM

½ cup (4 fl oz/125 ml) heavy (double) cream

2 tablespoons confectioners' (icing) sugar

2 teaspoons orange liqueur

honey and nut tart

❖ Preheat the oven to 375°F (190°C/Gas Mark 4). For the pastry, make as directed, adding the ground pecans to the flour before mixing.

❖ On a lightly floured surface, roll the dough out to a 13-inch (33-cm) circle. Ease the pastry into an 11-inch (28-cm) tart pan with a removable base. Press the pastry into the fluted sides of the pan and trim it even with the top edge. Prick the pastry base a few times with a fork. Line the pastry shell with a double thickness of foil and bake for 10 minutes. Remove the foil and bake for 5–10 minutes more, or until the pastry is light brown. Cool the pastry in the pan on a wire rack. Reduce the oven temperature to 350°F (180°C/Gas Mark 4).

❖ For the filling, beat the eggs lightly with a rotary beater or wire whisk in a medium mixing bowl. Stir in the brown sugar, honey, butter, orange zest, and, if using, orange liqueur. Mix well. Stir in the mixed nuts. Pour the filling into the pastry shell and bake for 25–30 minutes, or until the center is just set. Cool on a wire rack. Serve warm or cool.

❖ For the orange whipped cream, beat the cream, sugar, and orange liqueur together until soft peaks form. Serve immediately with the tart.

pastry for **single-crust pie**

1 cup (5 oz/155 g) all-purpose (plain) flour

¼ teaspoon salt

⅓ cup (3 oz/90 g) shortening or cold butter

3–4 tablespoons water

❖ Combine the flour and salt in a mixing bowl. Cut in the shortening until the pieces are the size of small peas. Sprinkle 1 tablespoon of the water over part of the mixture; gently toss with a fork. Push to the side of the bowl. Repeat until all is moistened (you may not need all the water). Form the dough into a ball. (If desired, chill for 1–24 hours.)

❖ To prepare pastry in a food processor, fit steel blade and process flour, salt, and shortening with on/off pulses until most of the mixture resembles fine crumbs but a few larger pieces remain. With machine running, quickly add 3 tablespoons water through the feed tube. Stop processor as soon as all water is added. Scrape down sides. Process with 2 on/off pulses (mixture may not all be moistened). Remove from the bowl and shape into a ball. (Chill for 1–24 hours.)

❖ On a lightly floured surface, flatten the dough with your hands. Roll out from the center to the edges, forming a round about 12 inches (30 cm) in diameter (or as indicated in the recipe). Wrap the pastry around the rolling pin and unroll onto a 9-inch (23-cm) pie plate (or as indicated in the recipe). Or fold pastry into quarters, place in the pie plate, and unfold. Ease the pastry into the pie plate, being careful not to stretch it. Trim to ½ inch (1 cm) beyond the edge of the pie plate; fold extra pastry under. Crimp edge, if desired. Bake as directed in recipe.

❖ For a fully baked pastry shell, preheat the oven to 450°F (220°C/Gas Mark 6). Prepare as above, but prick bottom and sides of crust all over with a fork. Line pastry shell with a double thickness of foil and weight with dried beans. Bake for 8 minutes. Remove beans and foil and bake for 5–6 minutes longer, or until golden. Cool on a rack.

caramel-apple pie

CARAMEL SAUCE

½ cup (3½ oz/100 g) packed brown sugar

1 tablespoon cornstarch (cornflour)

¼ cup (2 fl oz/60 ml) water

⅓ cup (2½ fl oz/80 ml) half-and-half (half cream) or light (single) cream

2 tablespoons light corn syrup

1 tablespoon butter or margarine

½ teaspoon vanilla extract (essence)

PIE

½ cup (4 oz/125 g) sugar

3 tablespoons all-purpose (plain) flour

¼ teaspoon ground cinnamon

⅛ teaspoon grated nutmeg

6 medium cooking apples, peeled and thinly sliced (about 6 cups)

½ cup (2 oz/60 g) raisins

½ cup (4 fl oz/125 ml) Caramel Sauce (above)

Pastry for Double-crust Pie (page 295)

PASTRY CUTOUTS (OPTIONAL)

1 egg yolk

¼ teaspoon water

3–4 drops red food coloring

3–4 drops green food coloring

❖ For the caramel sauce, mix the brown sugar, cornstarch, and water to a paste in a small, heavy saucepan. Stir in the half-and-half and light corn syrup. Cook and stir until bubbly (the mixture may appear to be curdled). Cook, stirring, for 2 minutes more. Remove from the heat; stir in the butter and vanilla. Cover the surface and allow to cool, without stirring.

❖ For the pie, combine the sugar, flour, cinnamon, and nutmeg in a large mixing bowl. Add the apples and raisins. Pour ½ cup (4 fl oz/125 ml) of the caramel sauce over the apple mixture (reserve the remaining sauce to serve with the pie). Toss gently until the apple slices are coated.

❖ Prepare and roll out the pastry as directed. Line a 9-inch (23-cm) pie plate with half of the pastry and trim the pastry even with rim. Spoon in the filling, top with the remaining pastry round, and cut slits for vents near the center. Trim and crimp the edge of the pastry to seal. Brush the top crust with water.

❖ Preheat the oven to 375°F (190°C/Gas Mark 4). If making pastry cutouts, use a small sharp knife to cut out apple and leaf shapes from the pastry scraps. Arrange on top of the top crust. Mix the egg yolk with ¼ teaspoon of water and divide mixture in half. Add red food coloring to one half and green food coloring to the other half; mix each color well. With a small, clean paintbrush, paint the pastry cutouts with 2 coats of egg mixture.

❖ Cover the edge of the pie with foil to prevent overbrowning, and bake for 25 minutes. Remove the foil and bake for 20–25 minutes more, or until the top is golden and the apple filling is tender. Cool on a rack. Serve warm or cool, with custard, cream, or ice cream.

pineapple-rhubarb pie

serves 8

1 can (20 oz/625 g)
crushed pineapple
(juice pack)

2 cups (8 oz/250 g)
sliced fresh or
frozen rhubarb

1 cup (8 oz/250 g)
white sugar

¼ cup (1½ oz/45 g)
all-purpose
(plain) flour

1 tablespoon
lemon juice

Pastry for Double-crust
Pie (page 295)

¼ cup (2 oz/60 g)
sifted superfine
(caster) sugar

❖ Drain the pineapple, reserving 1 tablespoon of the juice. Combine the pineapple, rhubarb, sugar, flour, and lemon juice in a large mixing bowl. (If using frozen rhubarb, let mixture stand for 15–20 minutes, or until the rhubarb is partly thawed but still icy.)

❖ Preheat the oven to 375°F (190°C/Gas Mark 4). Prepare and roll out the pastry as directed. Line a 9-inch (23-cm) pie plate with the larger portion of the pastry. Spoon in the filling and trim the pastry even with rim. Place the top crust on the filling and cut slits near the center. Trim and crimp the edge of the pastry to seal.

❖ To prevent overbrowning, cover the edge of the pie with foil. Bake for 25 minutes (50 minutes for frozen rhubarb). Remove the foil and bake for 25–30 minutes more, or until the top is golden.

❖ In a small mixing bowl, combine the superfine sugar with enough of the reserved pineapple juice (1–2 teaspoons) to make a glaze of drizzling consistency. Drizzle the glaze over the hot pie and cool on a rack. Serve warm or cool.

pastry for double-crust pie

For a version of this pastry made in a food processor, see page 277.

1²⁄₃ cups (8 oz/250 g) all-purpose (plain) flour

¹⁄₂ teaspoon salt

²⁄₃ cup (5 oz/155 g) shortening or cold butter

2–3 fl oz (60–90 ml) chilled water

❖ Stir the flour and salt together in a mixing bowl. Cut in the shortening until the pieces are the size of small peas. Sprinkle 1 tablespoon of the water over part of the mixture; gently toss with a fork. Push to the side of the bowl. Repeat until all is moistened (you may not need all the water). Form the dough into two balls, one slightly larger than the other. (If desired, chill for 1–24 hours.)

❖ On a lightly floured surface, flatten the larger ball of dough with your hands. Roll out from the center to edges, forming a circle about 12 inches (30 cm) in diameter (or as indicated in the recipe). Wrap pastry around rolling pin. Unroll onto a 9-inch (23-cm) pie plate (or as indicated in recipe). Or, fold pastry into quarters, place in pie plate, and unfold. Ease pastry into pie plate, being careful not to stretch it. Trim neatly and proceed with filling pie and adding top crust as directed in recipe.

spiced blueberry *pie*

serves 8

*1/2 cup (4 oz/125 g)
sugar, plus extra
for sprinkling*

*1/3 cup (2 1/2 oz/75 g)
packed brown sugar*

*1/3 cup (1 1/2 oz/45 g)
cornstarch (cornflour)*

*1 teaspoon finely grated
lemon zest*

*1/2 teaspoon
ground cinnamon*

1/4 teaspoon ground allspice

dash of ground cloves

*6 1/2 cups (1 lb/500 g) fresh
or frozen blueberries*

*Pastry for Double-crust Pie
(page 295)*

milk

❖ Combine the two sugars with the cornstarch, lemon zest, cinnamon, allspice, and cloves in a large mixing bowl. Add blueberries and toss gently until they are coated. (If using frozen berries, let stand for 15–30 minutes, or until berries are partly thawed but still icy.)

❖ Preheat the oven to 375°F (190°C/Gas Mark 4). Prepare and roll out the larger portion of pastry as directed and line a 9-inch (23-cm) pie plate. Stir berry mixture and spoon into the pastry-lined pie plate. Place the top crust on the filling and cut slits near the center. Trim and crimp edge of pastry to seal. Brush crust with milk and sprinkle with sugar.

❖ To prevent overbrowning, cover the edge of the pie with foil. Bake for 25 minutes (50 minutes for frozen berries). Remove foil and bake for 20–25 minutes more for fresh berries (20–30 minutes for frozen berries), or until the top is golden. Cool on a rack.

apple pancake stack

1 cup (5 oz/155 g) all-purpose (plain) flour

1 egg, plus 1 egg yolk

1¼ cups (10 fl oz/310 ml) full-cream milk

1½ tablespoons (¾ oz/20 g) melted butter, plus extra melted butter for greasing

1 cup (3 oz/90 g) flaked almonds

5 small green apples, peeled and cored

½ cup (3½ oz/100 g) brown sugar

4 oz (125 g) amaretti biscuits, roughly crushed

purchased butterscotch or caramel sauce, to serve

❖ Grease a 5-cup (40-fl oz/1.25-l) heatproof soufflé dish or bowl that will fit into the slow cooker.

❖ Make foil handles to aid removal of the dish after cooking by cutting three 18- x 2-inch (45- x 5-cm) strips of heavy-duty foil or regular foil folded to a double thickness. Crisscross the foil strips in a spoke design over the base and up the sides of the slow cooker.

❖ Process the flour, egg, egg yolk, and half the milk in a food processor for 10 seconds, or until smoothly blended.

apple pancake stack

✧ Add the remaining milk and the measured melted butter. Pour into a jug, cover, and allow to rest for 20 minutes.

✧ Meanwhile, toast the flaked almonds on low under a broiler (griller) for 2–3 minutes, turning until evenly lightly browned.

✧ Heat a pancake (crêpe) pan and brush with a little butter. Pour ¼ cup (2 fl oz/60 ml) of the batter into the pan and spread the batter to fit the circumference of the prepared dish. Cook until lightly golden, then turn and cook the other side. Remove to a side plate. Repeat with the remaining batter to make about 8 pancakes.

✧ Cut the apples into thin slices and place on a large tray, sprinkle with the brown sugar, and toss the apples to coat with the sugar.

✧ Place one pancake in the prepared dish. Spread evenly with a layer of sliced apple, then sprinkle with a little of the flaked almond and crushed amaretti biscuit. Continue to layer with the apple, almonds, amaretti, and pancakes, finishing with a pancake.

✧ Cover the dish securely with buttered foil. Lower the dish into the slow cooker and pour in enough boiling water around the dish to come halfway up the sides. Put on the lid and cook on Low for 4–6 hours, or until the apple is tender. Use the foil handles to remove the dish. Serve hot or warm with butterscotch or caramel sauce.

cherry-berry
lattice pie

serves 8

1–1¼ cups
(8–10 oz/250–315 g)
sugar

⅓ cup (2 oz/60 g)
all-purpose (plain) flour

3 cups (12 oz/375 g)
fresh or frozen red
raspberries

2 cups (about
13 oz/400 g) fresh or
frozen tart cherries,
unsweetened, pitted

¼ teaspoon almond
extract

Pastry for Double-crust
Pie (page 295)

❖ Combine sugar and flour in a large mixing bowl. Combine fruit and toss with almond extract. (If using frozen fruit, stand for 15–30 minutes, or until fruit is partly thawed but still icy.)

❖ Preheat the oven to 375°F (190°C/Gas Mark 4). Prepare and roll out pastry as directed. Line a 9-inch (23-cm) pie plate with one portion of pastry. Stir filling and spoon into pie crust.

❖ Roll out remaining dough portion to a 10-inch (25-cm) round. Using a fluted or plain pastry wheel, cut into strips ½ inch (1 cm) wide. Make a decorative lattice with the strips, trimming off any overhang, and pressing the strips against the rim to secure them. Cover edge of pie with foil to prevent overbrowning. Bake for 25 minutes for fresh fruit (50 minutes for frozen fruit). Remove foil and bake for 20–25 minutes more for fresh fruit (20–30 minutes for frozen fruit), or until the top is golden. Cool on a rack.

shaker-style lemon pie

serves 8

2 cups (16 oz/500 g) sugar

*⅓ cup (2 oz/60 g)
all-purpose (plain) flour*

⅛ teaspoon salt

⅔ cup (5 fl oz/160 ml) water

*2 tablespoons butter
or margarine, melted*

3 lightly beaten eggs

2 teaspoons grated lemon zest

*2 lemons, peeled, very thinly
sliced, and seeded*

*Pastry for Double-crust Pie
(page 295)*

sifted superfine (caster) sugar

❖ Combine sugar, flour, and salt in a large mixing bowl. Stir in water, butter, eggs, and lemon zest until well combined. Gently stir in lemon slices.

❖ Preheat the oven to 400°F (200°C/Gas Mark 5). Prepare and roll out pastry as directed. Line a 9-inch (23-cm) pie plate with half the pastry. Spoon filling into pastry-lined plate; trim pastry even with rim. Place remaining pastry over the filling and cut slits near the center. Trim and crimp edge of pastry to seal.

❖ To prevent overbrowning, cover edge of pie with foil. Bake for 25 minutes. Remove foil and bake for 10–15 minutes more, or until the top is golden. Cool on a rack. Dust with superfine sugar and serve warm or cold. Can be stored, covered, in the refrigerator.

apple-cranberry pie

serves 8

1 cup (5 oz/150 g) cranberries

¾ cup (6 oz/185 g) sugar,
plus ½ cup (4 oz/125 g) extra

2 tablespoons apple cider,
apple juice, or orange juice

3 tablespoons cornstarch
(cornflour)

1 teaspoon mixed spice

1 teaspoon finely grated
orange zest

5 medium cooking apples,
peeled and thinly sliced
(about 5 cups)

Pastry for Double-crust Pie
(page 295)

milk

sugar, for sprinkling

◈ Combine the cranberries with the ¾ cup (6 oz/185 g) sugar, the apple cider, and 1 tablespoon cornstarch in a small saucepan. Bring to the boil and simmer, stirring frequently, for 5 minutes. Cool for 20 minutes.

◈ Combine the extra sugar with the remaining cornstarch, the apple pie spice, and the orange zest in a large mixing bowl. Add the apples and toss to coat. Stir the cooled cranberry mixture into the apple mixture.

◈ Preheat the oven to 375°F (190°C/Gas Mark 4). Prepare and roll out pastry as directed. Line a 9-inch (23-cm) pie plate with one portion of pastry. Transfer filling to pastry-lined plate. Place top pastry over filling and cut slits near center. Trim and crimp edge of pastry to seal. Brush top with milk and sprinkle with sugar.

◈ To prevent overbrowning, cover edge of pie with foil. Bake for 25 minutes. Remove the foil and bake for 25–30 minutes more, or until browned. Cool on a rack.

pastry-wrapped
stuffed pears

serves 4

Tawny, slender Beurre Bosc
pears or golden Bartletts
work best for this recipe.
Be sure to choose small
pears with stable bottoms
so they will stand upright
during the baking.

1/4 cup (2 1/2 oz/75 g) orange marmalade

2 tablespoons chopped walnuts

4 small pears

Pastry for Single-crust Pie (page 291)

4 whole cloves

1 egg white

1 tablespoon water

1 tablespoon sugar

half-and-half (half cream) or light (single) cream,
to serve

✧ Combine the orange marmalade and walnuts in a small mixing bowl. Set aside. Peel and core pears, leaving bottoms intact. Spoon marmalade mixture into the center of each pear.

✧ Prepare pastry as directed, but roll the dough out to about a 13-inch (33-cm) square. Trim pastry to a 12-inch (30-cm) square. Use a fluted pastry wheel or knife to cut the dough into 12 strips, each ¾ inch (2 cm) wide, and 2 strips, each 1½ inches (3 cm) wide. Pat the pears dry with paper towels. Using one of the ¾-inch (2-cm) pastry strips and starting ½ inch (1 cm) above the base of a pear, wrap pastry strip around pear (do not cover the bottom of the pear). Moisten the end of the strip and seal to the end of a second pastry strip. Complete wrapping the pear with a third pastry strip to cover the hole and filling. Moisten the end to seal. Repeat, using 3 pastry strips on each remaining pear.

✧ Preheat the oven to 400°F (200°C/Gas Mark 5). With a knife or cookie cutter, cut leaf shapes from the wider pastry strips and mark veins on the leaves. Moisten the leaves and attach to the tops of the pears. Top the pears with whole cloves for stems. Stir the egg white and water together with a fork and brush onto the pastry to glaze. Sprinkle with sugar. Transfer the pears to a shallow baking dish, leaving space between the pears, and bake for 40–45 minutes, or until golden. Serve warm with half-and-half or light cream.

brownie crostata
with hot fudge sauce

serves 8–10

Bake this scrumptious brownie in pastry for the chocolate-lover in your life. Lay pastry strips across in one direction and then in the other to create an easy lattice top if the filling is too sticky to make a woven lattice.

BROWNIE CROSTATA

½ cup (4 oz/125 g) butter or margarine

3 oz (90 g) unsweetened chocolate, chopped

3 eggs, beaten

1½ cups (12 oz/375 g) sugar

½ cup (2½ oz/75 g) all-purpose (plain) flour

1 teaspoon vanilla extract (essence)

1 cup (4 oz/125 g) chopped pecans

Pastry for Double-crust Pie (page 295)

HOT FUDGE SAUCE

¾ cup (3½ oz/110 g) semisweet chocolate pieces or chopped semisweet chocolate

¼ cup (2 oz/60 g) butter or margarine

⅔ cup (5 oz/155 g) sugar

1 can (⅔ cup/5 oz/155 g) evaporated milk

❖ For the brownie crostata, melt the butter and chocolate, stirring frequently, in a small, heavy saucepan over low heat. Cool for 20 minutes. Combine the eggs, sugar, flour, and vanilla in a large mixing bowl. Beat until smooth with a rotary beater or wire whisk. Stir in the cooled chocolate and the pecans.

❖ Preheat the oven to 350°F (180°C/Gas Mark 4). Prepare and roll out the pastry as directed. Line a 9-inch (23-cm) pie plate with one portion of the pastry. Transfer the filling to the pastry-lined pie plate; trim pastry to ½ inch (1 cm) beyond the edge of the plate.

❖ Roll out the remaining dough portion to a 10-inch (25-cm) round. Using a fluted or plain pastry wheel, cut into strips ½ inch (1 cm) wide. Make a decorative lattice with the strips, trimming off any overhang, and pressing the strips against the dampened rim to secure them. Bake for 50–55 minutes, or until a knife inserted near the center comes out clean. Cool slightly on a rack.

❖ For the hot fudge sauce, melt the chocolate and butter, stirring often, in a small, heavy saucepan. Add the sugar and gradually stir in the evaporated milk. Bring to the boil, then reduce heat. Simmer over very low heat for 8 minutes, stirring often. Remove from heat. Serve warm over the crostata.

apple dumplings

serves 4

For a sweet surprise, spoon raisins, dried cranberries, dried cherries, or chopped dried apricots into the center of each apple before wrapping it with pastry.

SYRUP

1²/₃ cups (13 fl oz/410 ml) water

½ cup (4 oz/125 g) sugar

¼ teaspoon grated nutmeg

¼ teaspoon ground cinnamon

few drops red food coloring (optional)

1 tablespoon (½ oz/15 g) butter or margarine

DUMPLINGS

Pastry for Double-crust Pie (page 295)

4 small cooking apples, peeled and cored (about 4 oz/125 g each)

2 tablespoons sugar

⅛ teaspoon ground nutmeg

⅛ teaspoon ground cinnamon

ice cream or custard, to serve (optional)

✧ For the syrup, combine the water, sugar, nutmeg, cinnamon, and, if using, food coloring in a medium saucepan and bring to the boil. Reduce the heat and simmer, uncovered, for 5 minutes. Remove from the heat and stir in the butter until it melts.

✧ For the dumplings, prepare the pastry as directed, but divide dough into 4 equal portions and form each into a ball. On a lightly floured surface, roll each portion of dough into a circle about ⅛ inch (3 mm) thick. Trim each portion to an 8-inch (20-cm) round. Place 1 apple in the center of each pastry round. Combine the sugar, nutmeg, and cinnamon, and sprinkle over the fruit.

✧ Preheat the oven to 375°F (190°C/Gas Mark 5).

✧ Moisten the edge of the pastry with water. Bring the dough up around each apple in a bundle, pressing the edges together at the top to seal. Using a knife or small cookie cutter, cut leaf shapes from the pastry scraps. Moisten the undersides of the pastry leaves with water and place the leaves on top of the wrapped apples, pressing gently to attach and seal.

✧ Place the wrapped apples in an ungreased square baking dish, leaving space between them. Pour the syrup over the dumplings. Bake for about 45 minutes, or until the apples are tender and the pastry is golden. Serve warm, with ice cream or custard, if desired.

apple and dried cherry
strudel

serves 12–16

Traditional strudel dough
is rolled and stretched
paper-thin by hand. To save
time, use frozen filo pastry,
which is completely prepared
and easy to use.

Thaw filo pastry overnight
in your refrigerator for best
results when making strudel,
and cover the waiting sheets
with a damp tea towel as
you assemble the strudel.

½ cup (about 3½ oz/100 g) dried tart red cherries

½ cup (3½ oz/100 g) packed brown sugar

2 tablespoons all-purpose (plain) flour

½ teaspoon ground cinnamon

3 cups (about 1 lb/500 g) thinly sliced peeled
cooking apples

10–12 sheets frozen filo dough (rectangles about
18 x 12 inches/45 x 30 cm), thawed

⅓ cup (3 oz/90 g) butter, melted

1 tablespoon sugar

❖ Pour enough boiling water over the dried cherries to cover; let stand 20 minutes. Drain the cherries. In a large mixing bowl, combine the brown sugar, flour, and cinnamon. Add the apples and dried cherries; toss gently to mix. Set cherry mixture aside.

❖ To assemble the strudel, cover a large table or similar work surface with a clean table cloth and dust the cloth with flour. Unfold the filo dough and stack 2 layers of filo on the floured cloth, brushing between the layers with melted butter. Arrange another stack of 2 layers on the cloth, brushing between the layers and overlapping the stacks slightly. Add 3 or 4 more stacks, brushing and overlapping, to form a rectangle about 40 x 18 inches (100 x 45 cm). (Stagger the stacks so that not all the seams are down the middle). If necessary, trim to a 40- x 18-inch (100- x 45-cm) rectangle. Brush with melted butter.

❖ Preheat the oven to 350°F (180°C/Gas Mark 4).

❖ Spoon the filling in a band 4 inches (10 cm) wide across the shorter side of the filo, leaving a 4-inch (10-cm) margin from the edge. Using the cloth underneath as an aid, gently lift the edge of the filo and fold it over the filling. Slowly and evenly lift the cloth and roll up the dough and filling, jelly-roll (Swiss-roll) style, into a tight roll. If necessary, cut the excess dough from the ends to within 1 inch (2.5 cm) of the filling. Brush the top with the remaining butter and sprinkle with sugar. Fold the ends under to seal. Carefully transfer the strudel roll to a lightly greased 17- x 14-inch (43- x 36-cm) baking sheet. Bake for 35–40 minutes, or until golden. Carefully remove the strudel from the pan and cool on a rack. Serve warm or cold.

glossary

arugula (rocket)

Green leaf vegetable, with slender, multiple-lobed leaves that have a peppery, slightly bitter flavor. Often used raw in salads.

baste

To spoon or otherwise pour pan juices over food while it roasts, promoting moistness and a richly colored, well-browned surface. Baste meat or chicken regularly during the roasting time, especially in slow roasting.

blanch

Foods may be "blanched" to remove a strong flavor, to heighten the color, or to change the texture. The usual method, especially with green vegetables, is to immerse the item briefly in boiling water and then refresh in cold water. With nuts and tomatoes, for example, blanching makes it easier to remove the skin.

bouquet garni

This is simply a bunch of herbs that adds flavor to a dish. It is discarded before serving. The traditional combination is a sprig each of fresh parsley and thyme with a bay leaf, but it can contain a wider selection of herbs along with a few aromatic vegetables, such as the white part of a leek, a rib (stick) of celery, and a strip of citrus zest. Tie the herbs tightly together in a neat bunch with clean, fine string. To remove, snag the string with a fork.

coconut milk

A staple ingredient in Thai curries and used in beverages, sauces, soups, and desserts throughout southeast Asia, unsweetened coconut milk is made from water and coconut pulp. Rich and creamy, it is available in cans at specialty food stores. Do not substitute coconut cream.

couscous

This is a Moroccan staple, produced from semolina wheat formed into tiny pearls. Traditionally it is steamed for hours in a special apparatus known as a couscousière, but precooked or "ready in 5 minutes" couscous yields a very similar result.

deglaze

This means to dissolve the thin glaze of juices and browned bits on a pan in which food has been fried, sautéed, or roasted. To do this, add liquid such as stock or wine to the pan and stir over high heat, scraping up the browned bits from the bottom of the pan, thereby adding their flavor to the liquid for use as a sauce or a base for gravy.

eggplant (aubergine)

This versatile vegetable is available in several forms, primarily the large, pear-shaped Western or Italian type and the slender Asian varieties, which are more tender and have fewer, smaller seeds. Most are purple-skinned, but some are white.

When cooked, all eggplants have a mild flavor and tender, creamy flesh. Look for plump, glossy, heavy eggplants with no bruises or scratches. Will keep, refrigerated in a plastic bag, for up to 2 days.

frenching

Stripping the meat from the ends of the bones of a standing rib roast of lamb or pork and arranging the rack of ribs to look like a crown. This is usually done by a butcher. The bone ends are often protected with paper or foil ruffles for presentation.

nonreactive

The acids in some food can react with the metals used in some saucepans, changing the flavor of the food and introducing an unwanted element. Choose stainless-steel, glass, or coated saucepans for cooking acid foods, such as apples and tomatoes.

olive oil

When a soup recipe calls for olive oil, extra-virgin olive oil, extracted from olives on the first pressing without use of heat or chemicals, is preferred—particularly in regional dishes that derive some of their characteristic flavor and texture from the quality of the oil.

olives, black

Throughout Mediterranean Europe, ripe black olives are cured in various combinations of salt, seasonings, brines, vinegars, and oils to produce a range of pungently flavored results.

olives, green

Olives picked in their unripened, green state and cured in brine—sometimes with seasonings, vinegars, and oils—to produce results generally sharper tasting than ripe black olives. Green olives are sometimes stuffed with pimientos, almonds, or anchovies. Buy unstuffed olives for cooking.

onion, green

Variety of onion harvested immature, leaves and all, before its bulb has formed. Green and white parts may both be enjoyed, raw or cooked, for their mild but still pronounced onion flavor. Also called spring onion or scallion.

onion, red

Mild, sweet variety of onion with purplish-red skin and red-tinged white flesh. Also known as Spanish onion.

onion, yellow

Common, white-fleshed, strong-flavored onion distinguished by its dry, yellowish brown skin.

pine nuts

Small, ivory-colored seeds with a rich, slightly resinous flavor. Extracted from the cones of a species of pine tree. Use whole as an ingredient or garnish, or purée as a thickener. Also known by the Italian *pinoli*.

poaching

This is a gentle way of cooking food slowly in a poaching liquid such as water or stock. It results in meat or poultry with a rich flavor and velvety texture. The liquid should cover the meat or poultry and be kept simmering at just below boiling point so that the surface barely moves. Aromatic vegetables, such as carrot, celery, and onion, can be added to the liquid, which can then be strained off and used as stock.

radicchio

Leaf vegetable related to Belgian endive. The most common variety has a spherical head, reddish purple leaves with creamy white ribs, and a mildly bitter flavor. Other varieties are slightly tapered and vary a bit in color. Served raw in salads, or cooked, usually by grilling. Also called red chicory.

reduce

To boil a liquid briskly until its volume decreases, thereby thickening its consistency and intensifying its flavor. This is a simple way to transform cooking liquid into a sauce or the basis for a gravy.

rice, Arborio

Popular Italian variety of rice with short, round grains high in starch content, which creates a creamy, saucelike consistency during cooking. It is the preferred variety for making risotto. If it is unavailable, you can substitute any short-grained white rice, but the result will not be the same.

rice, brown

Rice from which only the outer husk has been removed during milling, leaving a highly nutritious, fiber-rich coating of bran that gives the grain its distinctive color, chewy texture, and nutlike flavor.

sesame oil

There are various types of sesame oil. Those made from untoasted seeds are pale and have a mild flavor; those produced from toasted seeds are amber-colored and have a very pronounced, nutty flavor. The latter is used in Asia, though less often for cooking than as a seasoning; its low smoking temperature and intense flavor make Asian sesame oil unsuitable for using alone for cooking. Most well-stocked supermarkets and Asian markets carry sesame oil.

index

Page numbers in italics refer to photographs.

C

D

a note on measurements

U.S. cup measurements are used throughout this book. Slight adjustments may need to be made to quantities if Imperial or metric measures are used.

acknowledgments

Weldon Owen wishes to thank the following people for their assistance in the production of this book: Stuart Bowey/Ad-Libitum (cover photography); Pauline Jackson and Sue Burk (loan of props); Nancy Sibtain (index); Suzanne Tawansi (digital image manipulation).

terrinelasa
gratincurry
risottobake
puddingm
marinateds
strudelspa